With the Ghurkas in Afghanistan

With the Ghurkas in Afghanistan
The Defence of Char-Ee-Kar
During the First Afghan War, 1841

Char-Ee-Kar and Service there with the 4th Goorkha Regiment
John Haughton

Notes on Goorkhás Including the Goorkha War & Types of Ghoorkha Soldiers
Eden Vansittart

LEONAUR

With the Ghurkas in Afghanistan: The Defence of Char-Ee-Kar During the First Afghan War, 1841
Char-Ee-Kar and Service there with the 4th Goorkha Regiment
by John Haughton
and
Notes on Goorkhás Including the Goorkha War & Types of Ghoorkha Soldiers
by Eden Vansittart

First published under the titles
Char-Ee-Kar and Service there with the 4th Goorkha Regiment (Shah Shooja's Force), in 1841; an Episode of the First Afghan War
and
Notes on Goorkhás

Leonaur is an imprint of Oakpast Ltd
Copyright in this form © 2010 Oakpast Ltd

ISBN: 978-0-85706-363-2 (hardcover)
ISBN: 978-0-85706-364-9 (softcover)

http://www.leonaur.com

Publisher's Notes

The opinions of the authors represent a view of events in which he was a participant related from his own perspective, as such the text is relevant as an historical document.

The views expressed in this book are not necessarily those of the publisher.

Contents

Char-Ee-Kar and Service there with the
4th Goorkha Regiment   7

Notes on Goorkhás Including the Goorkha War & Types
of Ghoorkha Soldiers   81

Lieut-Colonel John Haughton,
Commandant of the 36th Sikhs

Char-Ee-Kar and Service there with the 4th Goorkha Regiment

John Haughton

Contents

Preface	11
Char-Ee-Kar	15
Appendix A	52
Appendix B	55
Appendix C	57
Appendix D	62
Appendix E	76

Preface

It will be remembered by some who read this account that, on my return to England after the close of the Afghan Campaign in 1843, I was earnestly requested by them to publish a narrative of the events I witnessed, or in which I took part during that Campaign. It is desirable, therefore, to record the reasons which induced me to abstain from doing so then; as also those by which I have been influenced, after the lapse of a generation, in compiling the statements here prefaced. Several narratives, some especially referring to the disastrous period of the campaign, have been published. One in particular, Eyre's Journal, contained an account of the defence of Char-ee-kar from the pen of my friend and companion, Major Eldred Pottinger, written while he was still held a prisoner by the Afghans; it contained some expressions which, had I been at the writer's elbow, he would doubtless have altered; but it was sent home for publication before we met.

On the whole, it was a fair account; though from the fact that the writer of it was wounded, while acting as a volunteer with the Native Artillery, within a few hours of his taking refuge with our garrison, and confined to his bed till we were about to retreat, it was impossible he could be perfectly informed of all that took place at that time. I was not ambitious of parading my name before the public, and I knew very well that if I wrote a full and true account, with such comments as I should then have felt bound to make, if writing for public information, I should hurt the feelings of the friends of many deceased brother officers, raise a nest of hornets about my own ears, and enter an arena of literary strife, for which I was unsuited by habit and inclination. For these reasons I remained silent.

Since then, from time to time, writers who had occasion to refer to Char-ee kar, have frequently made the mistake of attributing the defence of that post to Eldred Pottinger; but this has generally occurred in a way which I could only meet publicly by a lengthy narrative, and on one notable occasion by appearing to side with my gallant comrade's enemies. I have more than once privately remonstrated, and received promise of justice, as usual in such cases, to be meted out to me at a future time. Last year Mr. Kaye, in his memoir of Pottinger, published I think in *Good Words*, again alluded to Eldred Pottinger as the defender of Char-ee-kar. I went to him to point out his error, and at his suggestion drew up the accompanying memoir, to be made use of in correcting his next edition of the War in Afghanistan.

While writing, I had occasion for geographical information, on a trivial point, on which my memory was at variance with Pottinger's published account; I applied to Mr. Kaye to obtain access to a map, believed to be alone accessible through his or some other official's favour. That gentleman never replied to my note. I have concluded, therefore, that it must have been consigned to his "Balaam Box," with that of the Emperor of Abyssinia—distinguished company, no doubt. The result is that (unlike the Emperor, having no opportunity of making reprisals), the labour of my pen goes to my private friends, instead of having the honour of furnishing material for the historian.

I have recently had access to a MS. Map in the Surveyor General's Office, Calcutta, which proves that my memory of the geography of the country is correct.

In compiling this, I have referred to Eyre's *Journal*; to an account published in the *Englishman* Newspaper in 1842 by Major McSherry, from dictation of Moteeram Havildar[1] of the Goorkha Regiment; and to a memorandum written by myself at the time, the last ever penned with my right hand.

My friend, Colonel Reid, R.A., has obligingly altered Moteeram's sketch in accordance with my memory; but it makes the place look more imposing than it really was. The extract of Major Robert Codrington's letter, in the appendix, more correctly describes the weakness of the position.

In conclusion, I must add that I have not the least desire to detract in any way from the high reputation of Major Pottinger, nobly earned. It will be seen from the narrative that to his chivalrous refusal to abandon me, I owe my life when wounded; but I wish to make plain that to Captain Christopher Codrington, and to myself after his death, the credit is due of having, as commander of the Goorkha Regiment, defended the post of Char-ee-kar. Pottinger's own letter in the appendix

---
1. See appendix.

ought, I think, to settle this, were it *disputed*, which in reality has not as yet been the case.

I have one more remark to make. Eldred Pottinger, in writing his narrative, naturally spoke of what had been done, as any one present would dot "We advanced," " we retreated," are natural expressions; but the use of the pronoun generally is not intended to convey the idea that the writer advanced or ordered an advance or retreat, but denotes the act of the writer's party. So when Pottinger says it was owing to my conduct that "we were able to hold out," it cannot be inferred that he meant to convey the idea that he was the commandant of the place; there are similar expressions in his published narrative, and I am not in the least surprised that, in the absence of anything from my own pea, casual readers were under the impression that Pottinger commanded at Char-ee-kar. I remember well that a portion of the English public imbibed the belief, from the frequent mention of her son-in-law by Lady Sale, (*Lady Sale's Afghanistan* by Florentia Sale, also published by Leonaur), that he was the chief defender of Kabool.

I have placed in the appendix the statements of two survivors of the garrison, unexpectedly met with since the narrative was penned, and also the printed narrative of Motee Ram Havildar. Numerous discrepancies may be observed: but memory is frail, and not to lie much depended upon in such exciting times. Had I been questioned immediately on arrival in Kabool, I could not have said how long our siege had lasted—it was one very long day to me. The circumstances I have stated have induced me to write of Char-ee-kar; perhaps, if ever leisure permits, I may pen adventures during the campaign, earlier and later.

Preface of the Second Edition

This pamphlet is reprinted almost *verbatim* from the edition privately circulated in 1867. I am now moved to publish it by the fact that the narrative by the late Major Eldred Pottinger, C.B., of the same event has been recently reprinted—*verbatim*, I believe—and consequently liable to the same misinterpretation as the original was. The appendices are given more with a view of showing that my statements are not exaggerated, than as being correct narratives of facts. Indeed, of two of the writers—Moteeram and Mohun Beer—it can only be said that their narratives, however interesting, contain much that is erroneous and confusing. My own account was made use of by Lieutenant Low (of late) I.N., in an article published by him in *Every Boy's Magazine,* in 1877.

Char-Ee-Kar

In the year 1839 the powers ruling India sent Shah Shooja-ool-Moolk to his native country, accompanied by an army composed of English and Indian troops, to secure his restoration to the throne of Afghanistan, from which he had been expelled thirty years previously, and which he had often since in vain tried to regain. I believe the original project was to seat him on his throne, and then leave him to his own resources, with the aid only of a small contingent of Indian troops, to be raised, officered, and drilled by officers detached from the armies of India. The plan did not prove successful, for, contrary to the expectation entertained, it became apparent that, however unpopular the former Ruler, Dost Mohamed, might have been, Shah Shooja was not a whit less so.

Some did not at all yield submission to him, and as early as the spring of 1840 there was a serious rebellion, also put down by English troops, in what is called the Kohistan; and altogether it was found that Shah Shooja could not get on without their assistance. We had garrisons at Kabool, at Ghuznee, at Kelat-ee-Giljee, at Kandahar, and also at Quetta, at the head of the Bolan Pass. The troops raised specially for the *Shah's* service were scattered about, and acted in conjunction with the others. The Kohistan, which General Sale had with much difficulty brought into order in the latter end of 1810, was thought to require the presence of troops to keep the inhabitants in awe; and a very small regiment was raised for the purpose and stationed at Char-ee-kar, the principal town of the district, under command of Lieutenant Maule, of the Bengal Artillery.

The Kohistan had a native Governor; but a political officer, with an assistant, and a doctor to attend to their health, were stationed in it also, with what view I know not. Early in 1841 the Native Corps raised specially for the purpose was deemed insufficient for "overawing" the inhabitants, and a regiment of the *Shah's* Indian troops, composed of Goorkhas, chiefly natives of Nepaul, was sent to take its place. These were further supported by two six and one eighteen-pounder guns, manned by some of the *Shah's* own gunners (Mahomedans, natives of the Punjab), under the nominal command of an eunuch of the *seraglio*, who, however, did not leave his more delicate charge.

Thus much has been said to show that the country, the scene of this narrative, was chronically in an insubordinate state. Dost Mahomed himself had only been able to master it by an act of notable treachery, so his countrymen reported. It is said that, under security of a solemn oath, he invited all the chiefs to a conference, and then murdered them. All the male inhabitants were used to arms, and usually carried them. In fact, it was an ordinary sight to see men at the plough with swords by their sides and matchlock and shield slung' at their backs.

The whole of Afghanistan is mountainous; it is, therefore, not easy to say why the country to the north of Kabool and south of the great range separating Kabool from Turkistan, should be called the "Kohistan," or Hill Country; but such is the fact. There is a high range of mountains shutting in the valley of Kohistan to the west, another to the north and east; and two low ranges of hills lie between it and Kabool. The valley varies in width, but is nowhere less than twelve miles wide. Although a large river, in many places unfordable, runs through the valley, collecting the waters of numerous streams, the general character of the valley is dry and sterile, cultivation being generally confined to the gorges and immediate foot of the mountains, as the soil, from its nature, does not retain water, and can only be cultivated where the supply is abundant. To be sure, some canals for the purpose of irrigation exist, but the turbulent character of the people is unfavourable to works of this sort, involving, as they do, much labour, and so easy of destruction as they are.

The inhabitants are for the most part located in castles, the walls of which are formed of mud, very solid, and able to resist the fire of small ordnance. Every landholder, or at least every family of any respectability, had one of these, and even in the towns of Char-ee-kar and Istalif there were several.

There were no wells in the country, the nature of the subsoil, containing (as it did) huge boulders, prohibiting it. The inhabitants were, therefore, dependent for water upon streams issuing from the mountains, or canals from them. These canals were generally lined with gardens and mulberry trees, and, on one side at least, had a hand of cultivation beyond.

Char-ee-kar was reckoned to be about forty miles, as the crow flies, from Kabool. It contained a population of, perhaps, three thousand inhabitants, and derived its supply of water from a canal which conveyed the waters of the river of Ghorebund. The head of the canal was said to be distant nine or ten miles. The town was situated at the termination of the slope of the western hills, from which it was distant about two miles. The canal from Ghorebund and the road to Kabool ran parallel to the mountains for some miles, dividing the cultivated country from the mountain slope almost devoid of vegetation. It was on this slope, close to the town of Char-ee-kar, that the Goorkha Regiment was stationed.

By ascending the slope a short distance, we could see into Nijrow, Gain, Bala Gain, and Doornama valleys on the opposite side of the great one, and distant from fifteen to twenty miles, which had either never submitted or speedily thrown off the yoke of Shah Shooja,

Amid the cultivation, not far removed from the canal, and about three miles distant from Char-ee-kar in the direction of Kabool, were a cluster of castles called Lughmanee. I believe they were the forfeited property of some native chief. There was located Major Pottinger, C.B., the political agent, who had earned a name throughout Europe and Central Asia by his defence of Herat. With him were Lieutenant Rattray, his assistant, and the doctor; he had numerous Afghan retainers, and a guard of Goorkhas from Char-ee-kar.

The Goorkha Regiment of Shah Shooja's force was sent to Char-ee-kar in the month of April or May, 1841, to take the place of the Kohistnee Regiment, commanded by Lieutenant Maule. It is time to begin a more particular account of this corps and its position The regiment was raised in 1838 at Lodhiana, in India, for the service of Shah Shooja. At first it was composed half of natives of the Himalaya, called Goorkhas, and half of natives of the plains. However, just before its arrival at Char-ee-kar it had been remodelled by substituting Goorkha recruits for the Indians. The great bulk of the regiment were mere youths, and fully half had never seen a shot fired.

The native officers and non-commissioned officers were for the most part very inferior. There were, however, some brilliant exceptions. Most were men who had for many years failed to obtain promotion in the Hill Regiments in India, and had joined Shah Shooja's service to get a step of rank. Somewhat less than one-half of the regiment had, however, witnessed the capture of Ghuznee, and a portion of them had done good service at Bameean in the previous year. The officers were Captain Codrington, of the 49th Bengal Native Infantry, who commanded it; Lieutenant William Broadfoot, second in command; myself, the adjutant; Ensign Salusbury, the quarter-master; and Ensign Rose, the subaltern.

There were also two European non-commissioned officers, Sergeant-Major Byrne, and Quarter-Master Sergeant Hanrahan. There were about sixteen native commissioned officers, and 742 rank and file. The whole were pretty well drilled, for the commanding officer had been himself nine years adjutant of a regiment, and added untiring devotion to his duty to a thorough knowledge of it.

When we arrived at Char-ee-kar, we had for months to live in tents; in fact, I occupied a tent up to the time of the outbreak. We found that Lieutenant Maule had commenced barracks[1] for his men, which we were to finish and occupy. A square of one hundred yards each way had been enclosed with a mud wall, and it was intended to build rooms against the wall all around for the occupation of the men. The officers' quarters were to be on one side of the enclosure, on the same plan, but of two stories. The houses were to be, like all in the country, flat-roofed.

My commanding officer and myself were at once struck with the indefensibleness[2] of the position, and I believe he remonstrated with someone on the subject, though not with the military authorities of the *Shah's* force. If he did, nothing came of it. We had to carry on the work after the original plan, and as far as I can remember, the only alteration made was the surreptitious addition of round bastions similar to those of the native castles. I remember this very clearly, as it was entirely opposed to the instructions Captain Codrington had received, *viz*., that he was to build merely a barrack, The sum allowed certainly did not exceed 600*l*., of which not more than 400*l*. was expended, a very moderate amount for housing between 900 and[3] 1,000 souls in such a climate. It was apparent to us that, in the event of an attack, water would he a great difficulty, but we were led to believe that such an event was impossible.

---

1. See Appendix B.
2. In a letter to my father, I described the place as charming, but observed, "I do not understand why we have been sent here, unless the Government are in a hurry to get rid of us."
3. Including camp followers, and women and children of the *sepoys*.

However, as, in addition to my other duties, I had to supervise the building and keep account of the expenditure, I did reflect very seriously on the subject of the water supply. We drew that for our ordinary consumption from the Ghorebund Canal, which passed about one hundred yards in front of our barracks, but a very small supply was also obtainable from Khojeh-seh-Yaran, a little valley in the hills to the west of us, the proprietor of which allowed the stream to trickle down once or twice per week to enable us to make mud for our walls. It occurred to me that we might either bring this stream down underground, or possibly discover another spring, and so conduct it; for it was palpable that an open canal above ground might be cut off at any minute.

I sent for the most celebrated diggers of "*kahrez*," as the underground conduits are called, who all negatived the possibility of such an undertaking for the reasons which forbade wells; and, as they justly observed, had such a measure been practicable, the inhabitants of Char-ee-kar would have resorted to it long since. As the only other measure we could adopt, we intended that if we could manage to save enough out of the sum allowed for building the barracks, we would construct a tank in the centre of the barrack-square, which would contain a supply for a few days. With this view we excavated the earth required for the works from that spot. It will be seen, however, that this place was destined to be applied to a very different purpose.

At the time when our trouble commenced, the barracks were partially finished. We had four walls, varying from seven to twenty feet in height, pierced by two gateways, east and west, with a row of flat-roofed rooms for the men all round the inside, except at one spot where were the officers' quarters. Unfortunately as yet we had no gate for the eastern entry, or doors for any of the rooms. The barrack square was built on a slope, so that its interior was commanded by the trees bordering the canal in front, distant about 100 yards. It was also commanded by the high towers of a castle forming the southern entrance of the town of Char-ee-kar. Its north, south, and west faces were commanded by a Mahomedan oratory and a butt erected beyond reach of our muskets.

In front, or to the east, the banks of the canal already mentioned, also garden walls, formed abundant shelter for an enemy; but in this direction, what was worst, was a small building beyond the canal, which we ourselves had erected as a mess house, and a stable on the banks of the canal in course of erection for our horses. There were also a low range of mud huts for shelter of our married *sepoys*; but these were built so as to be pretty well commanded from the barracks. Any one acquainted with military matters will see that our arrangements were as bad as they well could be. It is to be observed, however, that the slightly defensive character which our barracks took, was in opposition to the intentions of the ruling authorities. The most rigid economy was the order of the day, and had it been possible to select and make defensible a position (which it certainly was), I feel assured the proposition would have been negatived, and that the proposer would simply have brought himself into disgrace.

We had not been without some indications of the coming storm. Reports of a movement in the adjoining independent districts were rife. Thieves reputed to be from that quarter prowled about; not many days previously a shepherd was killed on the mountains near us, and his flock driven away. Thieves visited our own camp at night. My tent was pitched on the banks of the canal, and I had a guard consisting of a corporal and four privates and a bugler, it being my duty as adjutant to cause the bugle to be sounded for parade before dawn of day. One man was constantly on sentry, and the rest slept, on the ground by him.

One night a musket was stolen from beside one of the sleeping *sepoys*, and on another the bugler's bugle was carried off. These articles were paraded in the independent country. I received a message from an old *fakeer* to whom I had shown some favour, living at the place called Khojeh-seh-Yaran— the tomb of a saint—recommending me strongly to spend the winter in Kabool; and altogether Codringon and myself believed something wrong was going on. I know that he wrote to this effect either to Major Pottinger or his assistant, Lieutenant Rattray, and was answered by the latter that he might rest assured of full notice—twenty-four or forty-eight hours' notice, I forget which period was named—of any movement on the part of the rebels in the independent district. Captain Codrington handed me the note, and I put it into my pocket. When I lay wounded at Kabool, one day an officer came into my room, and seeing a number of papers, the contents of my pocket, lying in a recess of the wall by the side of my bed, said, " What have you got there?"

He began to examine the papers, and coming to Rattrays' note, said, "You don't want this; this is of no use to you," and there and then tore it up, and threw it into the fire. I mention this fact as a proof that Captain Codrington was on the alert, and would have been ready to put himself on the defensive if the authorities, under whom he was placed, had encouraged him to do so. The truth to me is plain, that no one in power anticipated any such outbreak as actually took place.

All my servants, with one single exception, were Afghans or Persians. One of the latter had recently left me. He was a native of Kandahar, and I have now before me the address he left with me: "Futteh Mahomed, to the care of Khan Mahomed Khan, in the service of Sirdar Poordil Khan;" the latter was one of the brothers of Ameer Dost Mahomed. It is possible that my servant, who refused to give any reason for leaving my service, may have had some inkling of the conspiracy brewing, but I think not. None of the others certainly had any, and they remained faithful to me

Thus much by way of a preliminary. On the morning of the 3rd November, 1841, some of my servants started on business to Kabool, They returned in a few hours, with intimation that the road was occupied by rebels from Nijrow, at a distance of some ten or twelve miles. This was absolutely the first intimation of the existence of any body of rebels in the *Shah's* territories.

After consultation with me. Captain Codrington proceeded at 1 p.m. to communicate this intelligence to Major Pottinger at Lughmanee, and to consult as to what steps should be taken in consequence. Major Pottinger being at that time the officer under whose orders he was acting. What follows, I take from a memorandum now before me, written on the evening of the 14th November, 1841; it is the last I ever wrote with my right hand. It concludes abruptly, for at the time drowsiness rendered me incapable of writing more.

At 2 p.m. firing commenced in the direction of Lughmanee. My first impression was, that it was nothing of importance, and arose out of an attempt of some of the hostage chiefs there detained to make off; but observing that the firing continued and that there were apparently two parties engaged, I deemed it my duty to send to the relief at least of my own commanding officer, who had intended to return immediately, and had evidently been unable to do so. There arose a serious debate in my own mind. Lieutenant William Broadfoot, the second in command, had returned to Kabool to act as secretary to Sir Alexander Burnes, who was to succeed Sir William Macnaghten.

There remained, therefore, only three very junior officers (ensigns) with the regiment; I was the senior in years and standing. If I went with the party I proposed to send, I should leave the regiment—now the most important charge—to the two junior officers. Again, if I sent either of the junior, and any failure took place, men might blame me for not going myself. I concluded that the best plan was to go myself; for, if successful, all was well: if I failed, the attempt would be evidence that I had not left a difficult duty to others.

At a quarter to three, therefore, I started with 120 men or thereabouts, in two companies. One great object I had in view was, to get down unobserved, so as to be able to ascertain the actual state of affairs before becoming engaged. Instead, therefore, of following the high road, I at once crossed the canal and marched through the cultivation, thus managing to reach Lughmanee undiscovered. Arrived, I found that the attack was mainly from the Kabool side. I rounded the fort, and then found that the enemy were chiefly occupying a large walled garden, into which I managed to get almost unopposed, one or two men only being wounded. These I was compelled to leave in a ditch, with injunctions to be quite quiet, till the affair was over.

The enemy was completely taken by surprise, and at once ran. The entrances to gardens are usually made so small that but one person can enter at a time, and he must bend double to do so. This is done to keep out cattle; thus before the enemy could get out, a good many were killed. The coats (padded with cotton) of several were set on fire by their own gun notches. I mention this, as a similar occurrence has given rise to statements that our troops had burnt the bodies of their enemies.

On our appearance the garrison of Lughmanee also sallied out, and the enemy were driven off at all points. Captain Codrington then strengthened the garrison of Lughmanee to 120 men, and agreed with Major Pottinger to send at dawn next day a supply of provisions and ammunition, which Major Pottinger was to send out a party to receive and convey into his castle. Our entire loss was ten killed and wounded. We got back about sunset; but before I finally joined Captain Codrington, one sad event occurred which troubled him much afterwards. There was a small village adjoining the castles, the principal inhabitants of which came out to assure him of their loyalty, they were unarmed.

Unfortunately as he passed, a shot was fired by one of the rebels from the direction of the village. This was attributed to treachery. Our men had, on hearing the report of the rebel shot, prepared to answer it. A raising of the hand and a wave of it, made by my beloved commander, settled the fate of six elders of the village, who lay dead as I passed. I know only of this fact from his own lips. I have never heard it adverted to since. It is highly probable that these people deserved their fate; for next year, many months after this occurrence, when I was a prisoner in the hands of the Afghans, a young man, to whom I had done a good turn once, was sentry over our party; he formed my acquaintance, and in conversation told me that the little village of Lughmanee lost thirty-three men on that day.

We saw nothing of the enemy on our way back to Char-ee-kar by the ordinary road, beyond noting that some still hung about on the road towards Kabool. We reached our barrack after sunset, and made arrangements for our own security, and the supply of provisions and ammunition to be furnished next day. I don't think I slept that night, or took off my clothes then. I know that sleep entirely left me for several weeks after. I only remember once attempting to sleep; it was in the daytime, and was unsuccessful. My usual post at night, when not moving about, was in a chair near the gate, where I soothed my wearied nerves with a *cheroot*.

Before dawn on the 4th November, the relief promised to Lughmanee was in motion. I started with several ponies, loaded with ammunition and provisions. I had with me my gallant young comrade and dear friend, Ensign Salusbury, Quarter-Master Sergeant Hanrahan, one six-pounder gun, and three weak companies of Goorkhas, or not more than 200 men. There had been heavy firing during the night, so that we knew that the enemy still hung about Lughmanee. It was good broad daylight as we approached, and I observed a considerable body, apparently seven or eight hundred, of the enemy on the slope of the hill to our right, among broken ground; this much embarrassed me. I had the most positive orders not to compromise my party or gun, I was to convoy the stores to what I may call the latitude of Lughmanee, whence, on seeing me, Major Pottinger was to detach a party to receive them.

The high road passed Lughmanee at a distance of about 500 yards; by a sharp turn to the left, a narrow lane enclosed by mud walls led to the castle. It was foreseen that if I went down this lane, I might lose my gun and possibly not be able to return. I was cautioned against doing so. I halted and sent Ensign Salusbury and two companies, with orders to turn up the party who threatened our right, and to draw down to my rear if they appeared too much for him, as, when they came out of the broken ground, I should be able to work on them with the gun. The enemy gave way, and our young soldiers pursued them only too precipitately. Bugles were sounded in vain, and orderlies sent out without result. At last, seeing no other means of getting the men back, and observing how the enemy were swarming from all quarters, I sent Sergeant Hanrahan with the greater number of my remaining men to bring them back.

All this time I had remained within five hundred yards of Lughmanee, waiting for the people who were to receive the provisions. They came at last—about ten horsemen, who, however, positively refused to return. Circumstances now rendered it impracticable for me to do anything but fall back on Char-ee-kar. When Salusbury rejoined me, the quarter-master sergeant and several of his party were wounded, and the firing had brought together the enemy from all quarters; the whole country seemed alive with them. When we commenced falling back, the men were disposed to bolt altogether, and it was with the greatest difficulty I could save my party by sticking to the gun, and with one or two faithful men loading it and firing it.

The enemy's cavalry charged us repeatedly, but as they were compelled to keep to the road, a round from the gun invariably turned them. Before we got over the distance, only three miles, poor Salusbury was mortally wounded, and our numbers much diminished. To wind up, when just within reach of the barracks, the trail of the gun gave way; but the enemy did not venture to close with us. We at once set about measures for our own defence. What provisions were to be had in the town were brought in; but as the shops and houses were all closed, it was not very easy to get anything, the more so, as we were ignorant of the places in which provisions were stored.

One of our first acts was to take possession of a castle which entirely commanded our barrack square. We were anxious to do so with as little offence to the owner as possible; it was necessary that he should not have the option of refusing us. Captain Codrington and myself, therefore, went to the castle, and asked to speak to the owner—Khoja Meer Khan, I believe, was his name. When he came out, we engaged him in conversation, while we walked towards our own barracks. It was under these rather unfavourable circumstances that I measured the distance, 450 paces.

The object we had in view was civilly explained to him when at the barrack, and a party of fifty Goorkhas, under a native officer, was sent over, and took possession without opposition. The owner, indeed,—I believed then, and do still—was well disposed towards us. The enemy now hemmed us in on all sides, and we had a day's desultory figting; we held, however, full possession of the gardens in front of our position. They occupied the town, and turned off the water from the canal; and we at once became dependent for our supply on what we could obtain from the pools left in it, and a very small quantity in a pit near the barracks, from whence earth had been dug to make bricks.

I gave the armourer directions for the repair of the trail of the gun, but eventually at night had to work at it with my own hands, he was no carpenter, though clever in his profession, and had no idea of the strength required in such a thing as the trail of a piece of artillery. We examined our ammunition stores as well as our provisions. Of the latter we had about seven days' supply. Of the former we had 200 rounds per musket—less the quantity expended during the previous day.

For the six-pounders we had originally sixty rounds for each, chiefly of round shot. For the eighteen-pounder we had only eight round shot and one 24 pound howitzer canister shot, which the artillery officer, who sent it out, specially explained, might "be altered to fit." This is ridiculous enough, but it is fair to say that the authority who ordered the gun out, only sent it for show, "for the moral effect." We had a considerable amount of old lead dug out of the target butt. This was cast into bullets, and placed in bags made by the tailors and women of the regiment, from the carpets of my tent, to serve in lieu of ordinary grape and canister for the six and eighteen-pounders.

Later, when this supply began to run short, we collected all our copper money, and the nails and fragments of iron in the armourer's shop, and turned them to the same purpose. They did good service, especially the bullets. Later still, when it was apparent that our bullocks would never be able to drag our gun, the drag chain was cut up into lengths, and bound up for shot. It made very efficient practice among the trees in front, so that the enemy's marksmen dared not occupy them. The chain cut the smaller branches like a knife. The blank musket cartridges, provided for the instruction of recruits, were broken up and formed into cartridges for the great guns.

But to return to our narrative of events. After a hard day we had quiet; and Captain Codrington (who honoured me, as he had always done, with perfect confidence, but on this occasion was pleased specially to approve of my services), desired me to write a report of what had passed, for the information of the military authorities of Shah Shooja's force at Kabool. He added that there was nothing I could write of myself that he would not sign. He had always been in the habit of writing his own letters on public affairs; consequently, for want of practice, writing was irksome to me; of course, I could not have said what he did in my favour in the despatch he subsequently wrote, and which I blushed to read. It was put in the postbag destined never to be delivered. I should value this document now more than any honour earthly power could bestow upon me.

After dark, when it was possible to turn our attention from our own immediate affairs to our comrades at Lughmanee, we sent our people in that direction for information. It was not to be expected that under our circumstances people would go unprotected to such a distance as that place; we could gain no tidings—our own people were utterly weary, and had to feed. Excepting the artillerymen, the garrison was composed almost entirely of Hindoos. I do not think that there were more than three Mahomedans in the ranks of the regiment.

The Hindoos would not, as a matter of course, eat food cooked by any but themselves or their wives, and, therefore, had fasted all the day. Had they been Mahomedans, one servant might have cooked for a large number, and while toiling and fighting, their food might have been in course of preparation. I strayed out after dark—I think it was about nine o'clock—in the direction of Lughmanee, with only an orderly with me, in the hope that someone might be coming in from that direction. I had not gone far when my quick-sighted companion saw people approaching. We were, of course, prepared for a speedy retreat; but were soon relieved by the discovery that the party consisted of Major Pottinger, the doctor, their retainers, and our own *sepoys* from Lughmanee.

Nearly all property had been abandoned. The doctor had across his shoulders the account book of the political agent tied up in a cloth; there were horses, spare guns, etc., but I think no baggage. I quickly escorted them into our quarters, where they were most heartily welcomed by Captain Codrington and Mr. Rose. We all sat down and listened with intense interest to their account of the events which had occurred, and which had induced them to abandon their own place. Our own extreme joy at having them with us was, however, quickly dissipated when we learned the fact that only a portion of our Goorkhas had returned.

For several nights I watched that road, in the hope that some more of our men would turn up. They did so as late as two nights after, and my joy was such that, on meeting them, I embraced them, as though they had been my own children. Europeans who have been in India are, perhaps, alone capable of judging of the exuberant feelings by which I must have been actuated, to indulge in such an unwonted demonstration of regard. Yes, I hugged them as though they had been my children. Having thus broken off from my story, I may finish all I have to say about them . They were men stationed on the towers of Major Pottinger's castle, who either did not hear, or did not understand the summons to come down, and who, though the castle was taken, kept their position without food or water till it was deserted by the Afghans, who would not venture to capture them by force, as their position was only accessible by a ladder and through a trap door. It is probable that the interests of the owner of the castle prevented their using fire to expel their enemy.[4]

Major Pottinger[5] has himself recorded the details of the defence of Lughmanee.

The 5th November was a sad day for us; we had a most severe struggle for existence, and though entirely successful, had to mourn grievous loss. Early in the morning the enemy mustered to attack us on all sides. It seemed indeed as though the whole male population of the country had assembled against us. I am sure that I am within bounds when I say that on this and several subsequent days, we were besieged by not less than twenty thousand armed men. Had they been at all organized, or under the direction of any man of ability, our destruction was certain.

An overruling Providence, however, made their numbers of no avail, and their utmost efforts fruitless. The very excess of their numbers gave us nerve; we also felt quite assured that relief would be sent to us from Kabool when our situation became known; and we felt that the mere interruption of the daily post would cause inquiry, even if Pottinger's messengers sent from Lughmanee[6] failed. We had not at this time the most remote suspicion of what had taken place at Kabool. The troops there were in no position to aid us.

On the night of Major Pottinger's arrival a discussion took place between Captain Codrington and myself as to the position of the

---

4. It is remarkable that they brought all their property tied on their backs.
5. See Eyre's *Journal*.
6. It would seem from Sir W. Macnaghten's unfinished despatch that on the 6th he received a hurried note written by Pottinger from Char-ee-kar. I do not know anything of this, but on the 6th or 7th I think he sent in two Goorkhas unarmed, with a despatch written in invisible ink between the lines of a native manuscript. These men got in safe, survived the campaign, and on my recommendation obtained the Order of Merit.

former, as it appeared not impossible that he might avail himself of his superior military rank to assume command of the garrison, which he had joined. We concluded that by rules of the service he could not do so: that we were still bound to act under his instructions as political agent in our intercourse with the natives, but that all military authority would continue with the officers of the regiment. I mention this, as the gallant major has more than once had the credit of the defence of Char-ee-kar. He did not require this addition to his laurels, and I have proof[7] under his own hand that he would not have deprived me of it.

The arrangements for the day's defence at its commencement were as follows:—I was sent to command the outpost in front. These were chiefly three walled enclosures, the largest of which contained two or three acres of ground. Pottinger volunteered his services, and was placed in command of the guns; Captain Codrington commanded and supervised the whole.

In the course of the forenoon I received a message from Codrington to the effect that Pottinger was wounded, and requesting me to come to him. Matters were too critical where I was to allow of my leaving. I therefore wrote him an answer, explaining the case, on a piece of cartridge[8] wrapper with charcoal. Our circumstances were these. The bed of the canal contained the only supply of water available, a little remaining in pools here and there. The possession by the enemy of the enclosures I have referred to, would entirely cut us off from this, and ensure our rapid destruction. It was therefore of vital importance to retain these outposts.

While I remained in any one place, all was safe there; but I was not long absent from any one position, before the men would gradually drop away, and the enemy would creep up and gain some advantage. Thus during the whole day we were engaged in a perpetual struggle to hold our position. I think it was about noon that I received intelligence of my beloved commander having fallen, and another summons from him; but it was not till near dusk that I could venture to leave my position.

How shall I paint the short interview which then took place? We were united by the bonds of the most sincere friendship and mutual esteem. The poor fellow was shot through the chest and scarce able to

---

7. Appendix A.
8. By a curious coincidence I met at Buxa, Bootan, since the above was written, an old *sepoy* who was with me at Char-ee-kar. and who mentioned this fact to me.

speak. He gave me his watch—which I now wear, but I could not find it, as it had slipped under him in bed; and when the stern calls of duty compelled me to tear myself from him, he sent a servant after me with his haversack, containing his telescope and pistols, etc. with directions to invest me with it. These touching proofs of regard at such a time move me to the heart even after this lapse of time.

Salusbury, who had been shot through the back on the previous day, had continued in a semi-conscious state, and expired this afternoon. We kept our posts in spite of the fatigue, caused by the extreme exertions the men had gone through and the frequent attacks of the enemy during the night.

On the 6th they attacked us with renewed vigour. The possession of the large garden in front was hotly contested, and the enemy early in the day got possession of it. I was not at that post at the time, but shortly after, hearing what had occurred, determined if possible to recapture it. I went up the bed of the canal, with a few followers, to ascertain the number of the enemy in possession. I had on the previous day caused a portion of the wall next to our barracks to be broken down, but for its strength I would have destroyed the whole. There was a gap about ten feet wide broken down to the height of a man's chest. Up to this I got, and from the silence within thought the place empty. I was soon undeceived, for I found it fully occupied and a sentry standing with his matchlock ready, a pace or two in the rear of the gap:

He at once fired at me, but without wounding me. In return I attempted to shoot him with a double barrelled pistol by Staudenmeyer, which, with its fellow, had cost me 30*l*. Both barrels missed fire. I then and there threw both pistols away, and trusted to my sword, the scabbard of which I had lost on the first day of the outbreak. As the enemy at once rushed up to the breach and I had only the Bugle major with me, of whom more hereafter, I was compelled to take ignobly to my heels; however, the disgrace did not rest long; having collected a sufficient body of men, I easily retook the place.

I note here that the enemy never stood when deprived of the protection of walls, even though they were ten to one, or the disproportion was still greater. We could not, however, attack them in the open plain, as our entire number was as nothing to the circle hemming us in. Later in the day I left Sergeant Major Byrne, a gallant soldier, in charge of the post; but shortly after he was brought in mortally wounded I took his place, the doctor and Mr. Rose defending the barrack; and the enemy having towards evening retired a little from our outpost, I went out, wishing to see if I could do anything towards the town. I had a very gallant little Goorkha orderly with me, we both kneeled behind the bank of a ditch looking in the direction in which we supposed the enemy to be.

We had been in our position but a few minutes, when we were enlightened as to the enemy's "whereabouts." My orderly[9] was, like most of his race, a little short man, his head and mine were both turned to the left. He was on my left side, a rifle ball passed through his head, striking me on the throat a little to the right side. We both fell: he stone dead, and I feeling paralyzed. I was not at all stunned. Our men, who were watching us, thought both killed; my poor orderly was dragged into the garden as men drag a wheelbarrow, the poor man's legs being used in place of the handles and his back as the wheel. The same process was commenced with me; but as I was alive and conscious, my objections I presume got me a lift at the head. I well remember that when set down inside, I came to the conclusion I was not "killed," that I sat up, and that when the enemy advanced again and there was in consequence a fresh alarm, I got up, took my part in their repulse, and forgot all about the matter.

When night set in, the combat was for a time closed. I went into the barracks, and there meeting the doctor, remembered that I was badly wounded. I learnt the sad news of the death of my beloved commander, and yet felt relief, as I felt it would have been impossible to move him in any exigency. The fact was kept secret, that the troops might not be disheartened. When I had the doctor apart, I told him that I feared I was badly wounded. He took me into an inner room for examination, that the disaster might not be known.

The doctor removed my neck cloth with the utmost care, opened my shirt collar which adhered slightly to my throat, and on looking burst out laughing, telling me I was not wounded at all! The truth is that partly owing to the fact that I had on an extremely thick silk neckerchief, consisting of a square yard of Mooltan silk, and partly owing to the obliquity with which the ball struck me, I had only

---

9. This man's case was curious: four of his brothers had been killed the previous year at Bamean, and he had at the same time received a bullet in the head, which, as there was but one hole was thought to have penetrated his brain; to the surprise of every one he recovered, but as the brain was injured, and only covered by a thin skin, he was thought unfit for further service, and only waited an opportunity to return to India.

received a severe blow on the front of the spine and an abrasion of the skin sufficient to let out a very little blood. There was a red mark on the skin, as though a finger smeared with blood had passed over it, and no more.

We were compelled to withdraw from the outposts in the evening. Our numbers were much diminished, and the men quite worn out with fasting and fatigue. To this was added the fact that we had now no water in the canal to protect, and therefore little object in maintaining the outposts in front of it.

At night secretly and silently a grave was dug on the east (or Nijran side) of a small building we were erecting in the barrack square as a magazine, and to it were committed the remains of my dear comrades Salusbury and Codrington. I do not remember when or where Sergeant Byrne was buried. My friend's grave was smoothed down, and straw burnt over it afterwards to conceal it, as I wished to keep the sad news as much as possible from the men. We passed the night much as usual, but this night and the following day there was an inexpressible feeling of relief from the fact of our having given up all our outposts, except Khojeh Meer Khan's Fort. We had in fact not more and probably much less than half the space to defend.

The 7th was ushered in as previous days had been, and as the remaining days especially were. I will for once describe it. As soon as it was broad day the enemy, in obedience to their drums which had been beating for an hour or two before, came forth from the town and formed a perfect cordon round us. There was a broad band on all sides, just out of musket shot,[10] from which the enemy stole out marksmen under cover of little piles of stones, as opportunity offered. The cover we had abandoned in front too, was completely occupied; also the target butt and the oratory.

It was now the *Ramazan*, and in the evening the enemy withdrew to break their fast, leaving heavy pickets of cavalry and infantry on three sides of us and in the gardens in front. In the course of the day we became aware of another loss. Shots began to drop into the interior of our square. At first these came palpably from the posts in front through the open gateway, and here I have to tell a sad tale which Mahomedans would consider especially illustrative of the doctrine of fate. Captain Codrington had a clerk, a native of Chandernagor in Bengal. This man was a Hindoo, and spoke English and French fluently. He was a very good man, but eminently timid. Regard for his old master

---
10. We had only "Brown Bess," with flint locks.

had induced him to come to Afghanistan.

When fighting began, he disappeared, nor did I hear anything of him till this time. I heard he was wounded, and went to see him. I found him crouched up in a corner of an inner room, that is a room inside another, facing the gateway. He had taken refuge here, as the most safe position he could think of. A bullet found him out, having passed through the barrack gateway, and the two doorways of the apartments opposite, into a remote corner. Another man, a tall, stout native of the Punjab, a Hindoo I believe, named Hassa Sing, *chowdree* of the *bazar*, or—to put the term in the most intelligible English I can think of—"Clerk of the Market" of the regiment, was also mortally wounded in the stomach, in a room a little to the north.

Pottinger who was in an upper room opposite to the gateway, was good enough to lend several rifles, his private property which he had brought from Lughmanee, to our marksmen, and I think it was at his suggestion that scaffolding was erected in his room and the upper part of the wall loopholed: also cover formed by boxes to shelter one or two men placed on the roof. The more immediate remedy adopted was to hang a curtain behind the gateway. We then fixed the eighteen pounder there, and filled up the space at the sides with the material provided for making the gate. But this was found to be a partial remedy, bullets penetrated the rooms on the south side of our barracks through the doorways.

The women inside were much alarmed, and the men on the roofs of the houses were killed and wounded. It was quickly found out that the fire proceeded from Khojeh Meer Khan's castle which commanded the interior of our square, and that our garrison there had succumbed. The only thing we could do was to put up the walls of the officers tents on the roofs of the barracks on the north and south sides, so as to prevent the enemy from taking aim at the men behind them. This dodge is known to the Japanese, and has been practised recently by them . It proved a wonderfully efficient expedient, and although we could not prevent some of the gun bullocks and ponies being killed, the arrangement at once reduced our mortality. Who would think of canvas stopping a bullet? It could not do so, but it stopped firing! Men would not fire aimlessly.

It appears that the *soobadar* commanding the Goorkhas in Khojeh Meer Khan's Fort had been talked over by the Mahomedan *Moonshee*,[11] a native of Peshawar, into surrendering. I don't blame ei-

---

11. Sent to act as an interpreter.

ther; the *Moonshee* was probably much better informed than we were of the actual state of affairs, and considered our case hopeless. The *soobadar* felt doubtless that he could not hold out. The place was too large in any case for efficient defence by fifty men without water; and forming, as it did, the side of a narrow street, it was easily mined by an enemy, who had cover up to the door. The *soobadar*, I believe, might have retreated to us with some loss, and in failing to do so only, I blame him; the place was untenable. He came over to us with some proposals for surrender, the reply to which was an invitation to the chiefs to confer. We had not heard of the cause of the outbreak, or the objects or wishes of the enemy, and hoped in any case to gain some information, all other sources being cut off.

On the 8th, two chiefs came forward to treat. They were, I believe, natives of Nijrow. I took them to Pottinger to confer with him, while I guarded against what we so much feared—treachery. I learned that Major P. had a long conversation with them, the upshot of which may be briefly summed up. They believed they were acting under orders of the King to expel us.[12]

P. said, "Produce the King's order, and we will at once evacuate the country." I know no more of this than I heard from Major Pottinger. The impression made on my mind was, that these men had been deceived, and had acted in good faith; certain it is that after this conference, the number of our besiegers was visibly diminished. I will now enumerate all the other attempts made to treat with us: all the persons who came were referred to Major Pottinger. One came on behalf of a chief of Nijrow or Tughao, and demanded guns, money, and I don't know what, to be surrendered. After Pottinger had had his opportunity of extracting information, I told the man that I positively prohibited anyone coming with such communications (which I perceived reached the men[13] and were most demoralizing), and I said, "If you do come, it will be at your peril. I will hang you."

Another day a chief, a genuine Afghan of bold and defiant manner, procured a cessation of firing, and forced himself in to have an interview with Pottinger, I don't know what passed. But it was plain to me he came merely for the sake of spying, I showed him round the

---

12. This is fully accounted for by the fact that documents forged by the rebels, but bearing the King's seal, were in circulation.
13. The men crowded to hear what passed, and those who could not get within hearing, questioned those who had heard—discussion ensued which was unsuited to our position.

place, told him I fully saw his object, and pointing to the bastion the Afghans had blown up, showed him how easy it was, and challenged him to come up that way if he could. He was the perfection of health and strength, but I don't think he quite approved of the spirit he found inside our place.

The last offer to treat was conveyed by the man I had promised to hang if he came again. I had then made up my mind it was impossible to hold out, and felt it would be an useless act of cruelty to put him to death. I, therefore, merely put him in ward, blindfolding him with my own pocket handkerchief, begrimed with the smoke of ten day's fighting. I regret that a Bactrian coin of Lysias, purchased a day before the outbreak, remained tied up in the corner. We felt, I believe, one and all, that it was utterly futile to treat with the enemy, and, further, when we came to know what had happened at Kabool, that it was our duty to hold out to the last, as our conquest would release the people who were besieging us, and leave them at liberty to aid those already pressing heavily on Kabool.

I think it was this afternoon we buried the dead. I most fortunately insisted on the doctor examining everybody before it was buried. One fine young man, who had laid a day or two with the dead, having been shot through the throat, was found to be quite alive and conscious. We buried forty-four in the great pit dug for a tank, but those killed at Lughmanee, on the retreat to Char-ee-kar, and at the outposts, lay unburied where they fell. Foolishly we would not bury the horses and cattle killed by the enemy's fire in the same place. They were quartered and thrown over the wall, in the hope that we would have an opportunity of removing them to a distance. This never occurred, and the stench became abominable.

We were subjected every night to the annoyance of false attacks, the real nature of which I did not know at the time. They were solely intended to wear us out. These facts I learned afterwards when a prisoner. One favourite plan was to keep drums beating for hours, and a large body of men in the bed of the canal in front, shouting, "*Dum-ce-Char-yar,*"[14] and other Afghan war cries. I afterwards learnt that these were chiefly unarmed peaceful men, residents of the town, who were compelled to turn out thus, sore against their will, while the bulk of the warriors took their rest. Eventually an occurrence took place which put an effectual stop to this.

9th. I believe it was on this day that all hope of relief was destroyed.

---
14. "The Life of the Four Friends;" that is, of the four companions of Mahomed.

About midday it was announced to me that a body of men were visible coming from the direction of Kabool. I at once went to look out, and saw them sure enough; but were they the relief long expected, or enemies? Relief certainly. I could make them out distinctly with a telescope. The foremost were horsemen, our own 5th Cavalry, a fact rendered certain by their white head dresses; we congratulated one another, and tears of joy streamed from my eyes; but, alas! it soon appeared we were deceived. The fantastic play of mirage had so acted on a herd of cattle grazing, as entirely to deceive us. In the evening a Syud, I believe of the family at Istalif, came in, and gave us the first news from Kabool, *viz.*, that Burnes was killed, guns (Warburton's no doubt) had been captured, and that fighting occurred daily.

The enemy kept us closely besieged. It was impossible on the east side for anybody to show his head without getting a volley. In fact, it was a favourite amusement to put a *sepoy's* hat (one of the old Belltoppers) on a stick and show it above the wall, and after the enemy had spent a good deal of powder and shot, to show them what they had been firing at, giving at the same time a derisive shout. Exposing myself incautiously for a few seconds, I received as I thought a ball in the elbow about the "funny bone;" my arm dropped so promptly that I did not doubt but that the bone was smashed. Taking off my coat, however, it appeared that the limb had only been struck by a spent ball, which left a painful bruise and nothing worse.

Here I may remark that we found the Afghans so short of lead that many of their bullets were only quartz pebbles covered with lead. This day I shored up the flat roofs of the barracks, and cut open the gorge of the bastion next the town, and mounted a six-pounder there.[15] The other one was brought into play down below. There was a heavy picket of the enemy's infantry and cavalry kept by night at the back of our barracks, between us and the hills, which entirely defeated a project for getting at night a supply of water from the Khoja-seh-Yaran spring.

The *subadar* of artillery undertook to dislodge them. He brought one of our field pieces to the side of the barrack square, furthest from that on which the picket was, and mounting the barrack roof, with the aid of a plumb line, he laid the gun in the same way that a mortar is laid, and elevating it sufficiently, fired over the opposite wall. Several shots were dropped in the middle of the picket, the men of which

---

15. It had been kept below for possibly service outside; the second one was not to be depended upon.

were just making themselves comfortable for the night. They were sent scampering, but only to take up a worse position for our interests, *viz.*, nearer to the coveted source of water.

In the evening some Afghans crept into the huts fronting the south-east corner of our barracks, and commenced singing vociferously. This was thought to be a piece of bravado. Some thought they were mining; I knew well they could not reach us before day, and that they would not venture to continue there during daylight, and that I could completely destroy their work at dawn if they were mining; so contented myself with visiting the sentries perpetually, telling them to keep a good look out.

In each of the bastions a *subadar* was stationed, excepting the northwest one held by Mr. Rose. I kept my usual post seated in a chair at the gateway, where I had a small reserve ready to act in any direction as requisite; the remainder of the regiment who survived unwounded were perpetually on duty on what I may call the walls—as many as could lay in each bastion; the others on the flat roofs, above which the walls rose from eighteen inches to three feet. The lowest parts were slightly protected by stones and billets of wood placed upon the top. After midnight there was a sudden explosion, alarm, and a general firing by the enemy. It appears they had excavated into the south-east bastion and blown up the front of it.

There was no mining from the huts, but a man had boldly sat at the foot of the bastion and dug a hole into it, which he loaded with powder, tamped and fired. The singing was intended to distract attention from his operations. The digging was distinctly heard by the women in the barrack below, but the *subadar* neglected the information conveyed to him. The men instantly deserted that quarter, and it was believed the enemy were among us, but I got together the reserve, and in a minute or two was in the breach. I found that it was unoccupied, and quickly barricaded it, so as to render it as strong as before

The enemy had made no attempt to take advantage of what had been done. Had they advanced with a storming party, the place would have been theirs in all probability, instead of which they merely indulged in a desultory fire. After this a piece of lighted port-fire was dropped over the walls at each bastion every half hour, so as to enable us to see what was going on below.

10th. Since the supply of water failed from the canal and we had been confined to the barracks, the practice was to open the Postern Gate, a small, narrow one, for a short time after dark, and allow the garrison to go out to get their supply from the pit, where it had been received for building purposes before the siege, and from the hollows round the walls where earth was obtained for their construction. This measure I had to superintend myself, as from the narrowness of the entry and the eagerness of the people, there was great danger of a crush, and much of the water was spilt. This evening the last drops of water remaining were collected in pitchers, and brought in and placed under sentries in a room.

11th. Water was served out to fightingmen only. At first, referring to the fact that the corps was composed entirely of Hindoos, I ordered a native officer to serve it out; but quickly a cry of partiality was raised, and the men insisted that I should serve it out. I did serve out water on this and the succeeding day as far as it would go, about half a tea cup[16] full to each man. Those who know Hindoo prejudices on the subject, and remember that every man, from the Brahmin and Rajpoot downward, lost his caste by thus receiving water in a tea cup from my hand will be able to realize in a measure the amount of suffering which the men had undergone to induce them to make such a sacrifice.

Yet all appeared staunch, I heard no murmuring. One of our Mahomedan gunners had deserted it is true. The rest, to be sure, had asked for their pay on the pretext that they had not the means of buying food at the regimental shops; but I had a plain answer: I had not received it; and, to obviate difficulty, ordered credit should be given them. I allowed them and the *sepoys* generally as much mutton as they could eat from the officers' mess flock; little was used, as they said it only made them more thirsty. I learnt afterwards that many sucked the raw flesh to assuage their thirst. Fighting is at all times dry work, but fighting without water is nearly impossible.

The misery was great; the Hindoos, accustomed to daily ablutions, had not bathed since the commencement of the affair. Even at the time that we were still unconfined to our barracks, food was only obtainable at irregular intervals; our voices were hoarse, our lips cracked, our faces begrimed with dust and smoke, and our eyes bloodshot. I do not remember to have sat down to a meal after the evening on which Pottinger joined us, my food being chiefly dried mulberries obtained from the *Fakeer's Tukeea* in front, or fried flour brought to me by the *sepoys.* Truly we were one.

There was, however, an article of diet without which I don't think I could have held out. Each morning before daylight Captain Co-

---

16. Much of this was mere mud.

drington's servant brought me a cup of tea. The last was, I think, on the morning of the 12th, and was from a small vessel of water which Mr. Rose had secured. This was the sole source of supply for himself, Major Pottinger, the doctor, and myself, and certainly for two days, if not three, beyond the small cup of tea I tasted no fluid.

In the evening I sent out a party[17] by stealth to endeavour to get a supply of water by passing between the enemy's pickets, and getting in rear of the town, to the spot where the water from the canal which had been cut ran down. They got a little water, but alarmed the enemy, and lost the greater part of what they were bringing in; what came was at once seized and drank by whoever could get hold of it. One or two of the party were reported to have been captured by the enemy.

12th. We were in every way, as might be supposed, much worse off. Since rain fell on the night of the 5th, the weather, especially at night, had become much colder, the mountain tops being covered with snow. Our men were almost entirely worn out, the enemy used all sorts of contrivances to dispirit us. Scaling ladders were for several days paraded round us, though in several places the enemy could get in without using them, as they could reach the top of the wall from the outside with their hands. There was usually one general attack *per diem,* and it did not fail today; many men were absent from their posts, and I had to drive them up from their barracks.

During the fight some slunk away again, and among these a native officer. I discovered him in the corner of a room, behind a screen, with fire in a chafing dish burning before him, mumbling "*Muntras*" or magic formulae. It was needful to make an example, so I pulled him out by the collar, tore his coat off, and set him to work as a coolie with the camp followers. We were attempting to fill up the unfinished magazine with earth, intending to convert it into a Cavalier, on which to mount our second gun, so as to command the breach made by the enemy in our south-east bastion. I was soon obliged to give it up, and admit the validity of the excuse made by the poor people, who said they could not work without water.

I organized an expedition to attempt again to get water this evening, and intended myself to command it; but the native officers of the corps conjured me not to go out, as they said, if anything hap-

---

17. This expedition was prompted by the fact that some had let themselves down over the walls, whence they had stolen to the back of the town and obtained water. The measure was so bold that, but for the success of these adventures, I should not have thought of it.

pened to me, they had no[18] one to look to for guidance. I felt compelled to give in, and yet, feeling the absolute necessity of keeping the men in strict control, I placed the expedition under the orders of Mr. Rose and our best native officer. I indicated the points they were to hold till the water carriers returned, and did all in my power to ensure success. The urgent necessity for absolute silence was pointed out to all, and I had good hope that we might succeed in getting enough water to last for a day or two.

After a long and anxious interval we were amazed by firing close to us—a volley at the building intended for a mess house and another at the canal, followed by scattered firing in the same direction, and then from the enemy's pickets. By-and-bye the detachment returned, rampant with triumph, but without water, or scarcely any. Whatever quantity came was at once consumed or disposed of privately. Rose brought two standards captured from the enemy. The first thing I learnt was, that my plan had entirely failed. The posts indicated by me were not taken up, which, considering that all were suffering the agonies of thirst, was not to be wondered at. All rushed to the water, which was reached without detection, they then drank their fill, and instead of following up the plan laid down, which might still have been adopted in part, conceived the idea of falling on the pickets of the enemy in front of our position.

This view was carried out, and I believe the picket at the mess house and at the canal were attacked at the same time. It was found that the whole of them had gone to sleep, without planting a sentry; they were in fact enjoying their first sleep after a day's hard work and a heavy meal, for it was now the *Ramzan*, during which they fasted all day till the sun went down. Poor people! to the majority it was also their last sleep. I was told that the mess house being surrounded and aim being taken, the first volley was fired, and those not killed by it were bayoneted.

Almost simultaneously a similar event took place at the canal, the party near which were chiefly mere "*claqueurs*," driven there to annoy us by yells: some of these escaped. However, the enemy received a terrible blow, but the success appeared to me quite useless. The object for which the party was sent forth had entirely failed, and we were dying of thirst. I had a horror of the destruction of even such men as the Afghans were by such means. It seemed unmanly. To be sure they would

---

18. The only remaining officer of the regiment, Mr. Rose, was very young; he had joined the service but a few months previously.

only have been too glad to treat us in the same way, if they[19] could. Our black[20] bearded visitor who was a chief of some distinction, was among the dead; great lamentation was made over him next day.

13th. The failure of our attempts to obtain water, except for the few who went forth, made it manifest we could no longer hold out. All the hope we ever had of. relief from Kabool had long since vanished; and it was clear we must either die where we were or effect some change in our circumstances. As our position was palpably untenable, the probability of having to effect a retreat had been often in our minds from the first; but it was combined with the hope of assistance from Kabool; for no one needed to be told that a retreat over from forty to fifty miles of country in open rebellion was impossible to people so outnumbered that they could not show their noses outside their barracks.

We had no means of carrying our wounded, and so early as the date of the death of the gallant Codrington I felt inexpressible relief from that event, as I was well aware that in the event of it being necessary to remove him, he could not bear the motion of the single *doolee* or litter we had for carrying the wouuded. There were a great number of considerations which negatived even an attempt at retreat till this day. In the forenoon, however, the native officers in a body came towards me. I had noticed whisperings and consultations in twos and threes among them and did not require any one to tell me what it meant.

As they drew near, I understood their errand only too well. They respectfully announced that "something" must be done," as it was impossible they could hold out any longer without water. I had quite made up my mind too on the subject, and in reply pledged my life on the attempt to lead them to water that night. Now for the first time a council was held in the room where Pottinger lay wounded, at which the doctor and Mr. Rose, I believe, assisted. The question of retreat or no retreat was not discussed.

The only alternative to my mind was to attempt to seize by surprise some native castle in which we might expect to find some food and have access to water, but I could not call to mind a single one from which the supply could not be cut off. All were agreed that our only chance, hopeless as it seemed, lay in attempting to reach Kabool.

---

19. I remember in the spring an English soldier was shot at night, as he lay asleep in his tent amidst his comrades at the camp at Seeah Sung near Kabool. This was done in the mere wantonness of hate.
20. Shah Mahmood.

If we got a good way, it was thought possible, relief might meet us and help us in. The route was the only question of debate. The direct route was the most difficult and one upon which opposition was most certain; for we had to pass several fortified villages, if we went by it. My own acquaintance with the country was imperfect, but I was disposed to take a line to the left or S. E. which, it seemed to me, would bring us into broken ground, where the enemy's horse could not act against us, and from whence we might possibly effect a junction with Colonel Sale's Brigade, supposed to be in that direction.

Pottinger and the doctor, who both had seen much more of the country than I had, were in favour of adopting a line of road skirting the mountains, as it would give, in the event of our being cut up, the best chance of escape to the women and children and camp followers, who might perhaps be able to clamber the sides of the hills and find shelter among the rocks. There was another recommendation to this route; it would probably be unwatched, and it abounded in water; we knew too that there were some well disposed to us in the direction of Istalif. I fully concurred in these arguments, and it was understood that we would adopt the hill foot route.

Our plans it was thought prudent to conceal as far as possible. Spikes were ordered to be made for the guns, but the armourer who made them, protested that they would not break, as he had no liquid in which to cool them. I suggested the use of *ghee*, not knowing at that time the effect of oil on steel. The doctor urged me to save my Bactrian coins. I had a valuable collection, which I could have conveniently carried in my pockets, but as I had adopted it as a principle that all baggage was to be abandoned, I could not in my own person set the example to the contrary.

After what has been already recorded, I do not think there are many persons who would want explanation of the state which rendered retreat necessary; but I will nevertheless briefly recapitulate our condition. On the 2nd November we had about seven hundred and forty men, more than half of whom were recruits, and who had never been under fire. We had since then lost our commandant, quarter master, sergeant major and, I believe, fully 100 privates killed; we had our quarter master sergeant and eight barrack rooms full of wounded, probably not less than two hundred, we had lost fifty by capture.

This is the lowest estimate, so that there could not remain more than three hundred and ninety worn out men under arms. We had over one hundred women and forty children, with perhaps one hundred camp followers of sorts. The whole of this party was totally destitute of water. At the commencement we had only by estimate seven days' provisions, but our store was by no means exhausted.[21] It probably would have carried us a week farther.

Our ammunition had been at starting 200 rounds per man, but had been husbanded with the greatest care; no such random firing was allowed as I have repeatedly seen since, and our store was therefore still respectable; we had but little ammunition for the guns, one of which had broken down thrice; and our muskets were so foul, that it was with difficulty balls could be forced into them; even urine could not be obtained to wash them out. We were closely besieged by overwhelming numbers, and could not show ourselves outside in daylight; all hope of relief had vanished; and to us remained alone the choice of death, surrender to a notoriously faithless enemy, or the attempt to join by stealth our comrades at Kabool, I had received from two men, the armourer and the native doctor, one a native of the Punjab and the other of Cashmere, hints that treachery was brewing among the gunners; but I could get no tangible explanation from them of the grounds for their supposition.

The gunners had behaved as well as men could do. They fought bravely, and had lost twelve men out of fifty-six, their entire number. As I then said, they were as my right arm to me; I could not therefore either punish them on vague suspicion, nor could I even turn them out of the barracks, possibly to increase the enemy's ranks, especially as their accusers had shewn no courage themselves. Indeed the native doctor was reputed an arrant coward. I did what I deemed right, and gave private instructions that a vigilant eye should be kept on them. The precise nature of our expedition to take place in the evening was for good reasons kept secret; but I had openly pledged my word to do something, and the necessity for making spikes for the guns, in anticipation of having to abandon them, would have betrayed our objects, if all were so dull as not to be able to form a pretty good guess. We never had draught carriage for all three guns, and as the bullocks had been entirely without water from the 6th, if not before, and altogether without food for five days, as indeed all our beasts were, it was hopeless to expect them to do service.

The armourer had just shown me the spikes, and explained his difficulty about rendering' them brittle, and a cessation of firing occurring at this time, I went up to the N. E. Bastion to see "what was

---
21. Chiefly from want of water to cook with.

up." Ensign Rose was with me, and also the *subadar* of artillery. I saw a native of India, with clean clothes and combed hair, coming towards the gateway. I asked, observing he was an artilleryman, whether he was the man who had deserted, or whether he was the man cut off in the attempt to obtain a supply of water. The *subadar* at once gave answer that he was the deserter. In any case it was plain that the enemy had sent him, probably to offer terms; and as I was quite determined not to make any, being completely assured that none made with us would be kept, I felt it of importance to prevent his holding any communication with the men

At this time I was unarmed. I met the man as he came in, and seized him by the collar with my left hand as he attempted to pass me. Instantly he threw himself on the ground, I still holding him; this reduced me to a stooping posture, in which I received a tremendous blow on the neck, which I conjecture was followed by one or two more. I started, letting go my man, and turning round, at the same time feeling a sharp pain in my right wrist; I saw the blood spouting in a long jet from it, and the *subadar* glaring at me like a demon, holding a sword with both hands, and in the act of striking at me again.

All this was the work of an instant. I had the whole of the muscles[22] on one side of the back of my neck severed, a severe cut into the right shoulder joint, another in the right wrist, nearly severing my hand, and a fourth in the left forearm, splintering the bone. I retreated up a ladder to the roof of the barracks, and shouted "Treachery," calling on the men to fire on the gunners, who were escaping *en masse*. I, however, after having the limb with its spouting artery bound, found myself so faint from loss of blood that I could not stand. I was conducted between two men into the lower storey of the building, in which was Pottinger, and was laid on a bed.

The enemy made a most vigorous attack on all sides. Pottinger had himself carried to the gate, where the doctor, with one or two men, vigorously worked the eighteen-pounder, and by dark the enemy had been completely repulsed. I heard afterwards that the artillerymen, seeing our affairs were desperate, thought it best to make terms for themselves. The arrangement was, they were to kill me as a proof of their zeal, and to go over to the enemy, who were to make a general attack in the confusion which would ensue, and take the place by escalade. It was expected no one would remain to work the guns; on

---

22. A bad tailor, who had made one of the most prodigious collars ever seen, was probably the unintentional means of saving my life.

this point, and in the anticipated success, calculations failed.

It appears that from some sign the *subadar* understood all was settled. He, therefore, when I left his side, snatched a sword from the hands of Ensign Rose, and followed me. I presume, when the man I had seized, whose face was toward the *subadar* saw him coming at me, he threw himself down to be out of the way of the blow.

Major Pottinger, the doctor, and Mr. Rose, after driving off the enemy, attempted to organize a retreat, but this was out of the question; none of them but Rose belonged to the corps, and he was too young and unused to command. The men, women, and camp followers began to load themselves with whatever they could find. A Goorkha *jemadar* served the cash[23] in the regimental chest out to whoever would take it. The doctor spiked the guns, and it was proposed to blow up the magazine, but I negatived this, for two reasons. It would be sure to arouse the attention of the enemy, and thereby defeat our attempt to escape secretly; and probably it would destroy our wounded, who were unable to move. I have said, discipline was at an end, but still there was some attempt made at order.

It was arranged that after dark the force should be divided: one half to leave by the main entrance, and the other half by the postern gate; both parties were to unite on the parade ground, and proceed in silence by the route previously determined. When all was nearly ready the doctor came to me. An assistant made a light with a piece of oiled rag, and the doctor amputated my right hand at the wrist joint, rapidly sewing the skin together with three stitches of a needle and thread. As may be supposed, I was dreadfully faint, but not a drop of liquid of any kind was to be found, some ether excepted. Tinctures of all sorts had disappeared from the Hospital, the smell of the ether luckily had been too powerful, and a drink of it revived me. I was put on horseback and led out by the postern, a man holding me on either side, to the parade ground.

There we waited unavailingly for the other party; a man was sent back to bring them on; he did not, I believe, return. While waiting, an infant began to cry; the doctor said he would silence it, and he did so for ever, I was told, by dashing it on the ground.[24] He went back himself in search after the missing men but did not return to us. At last we

---

23. The man's name was Hunooman Singa Jemadar. He had been from Nepal to Pekin with tribute. He measured out the money with a brass *lotah* or drinking vessel. He was a brave soldier.

24. This was confirmed by an eye-witness in 1871.

started, Pottinger leading. I continued to be held by a man either side of my horse, with a cushion under my chin to keep my head up. After travelling about four miles, we came to water. It was difficult to get the party to move at all from this, and I was told that many never did so.

Pottinger was fully impressed with the fact that in speed and secrecy alone had we a chance of escape; he therefore urged the party on. Rose and the Quarter Master Sergeant Hanrahan (who had recovered from the wound received on 4th November) were to bring up the rear, but this was found impossible. We waited and halted repeatedly, with the result of constantly diminishing numbers. At I think about 1 a. m. we heard firing to the left at Kalabagh on the main road, which I afterwards ascertained arose from the detection of the party which had failed to join us on leaving the barrack. I think it was some time before we got to Istalif, that we missed Ensign Rose, Sergeant Hanrahan and the men with them.

Pottinger's object was to draw them on as fast as he could, and to show the way, waiting occasionally in difficult places for them to come up. We had travelled about twenty miles, when we missed them, and all endeavours failed to discover them again.[25] It was clear that they had taken some other path, so having no choice, we pushed on, our party diminished to seven or eight. We stumbled on a water mill, with the miller awake and busy, he too readily came out with a welcome which we dared not return, but on the contrary avoided. We struggled on, continually losing our way in the dark till day began to dawn, when we found ourselves under the walls of a fortified village, beyond which was a naked hill.

The majority of our party were in favour of taking to this hill, for the sake of concealment, I felt very strongly, however, that when our evacuation of Char-ee-kar was known, the enemy would be sure to look for us in such a situation. I recommended we should take shelter in some ravines channelling the otherwise almost level plain near the village, where I felt assured the enemy would never dream of looking for us.

It was indeed fortunate that we did so for what I anticipated oc-

---

25. Pottinger feelings and mine probably differed. He had been nine days in bed and was consequently cool. I had been the whole of the time in constant excitement. He did not belong to the regiment. I did. Nothing would have induced me to part company with my men as long as they would follow me. He now looked upon them as what they really were, a disorderly mob, useless as soldiers. This is written with reference to remarks in his narrative.

curred; the enemy were seen hunting, and firing at some of our men on the hillside, while we lay at hand closely concealed. Once indeed a party came up to within two hundred yards of us, but turned back without seeing us. Our party now consisted of Major Pottinger, myself, the major's Goorkha[26] *Monshee* named Mohun Beer, all mounted, my orderly Maun Sing, and a regimental sutler on foot. I must not, however, forget Major Pottinger's bull terrier, of whose barking I was apprehensive when the enemy approached us, but who was, I was assured, too tired to bark.

During the night I had drunk water liberally, and I believe about half a pint of ether. During this terrible day the largest share of the little water with our party, was given to me. I had also some dried mulberries to eat. As soon as it was well dark, we pushed on again, Pottinger guiding; we passed close to Killa Iltifat, a castle where the dogs alone took notice of us, and crossed an open plain to the last range of hills dividing' us from Kabool. Now I knew of only two roads crossing it, both of which were sure to be watched; but Pottinger, who had frequently passed and repassed, knew of a goat path between them, but he had never trodden it, and in any case it would be a tough job for a horse to cross the hill by it. We pushed on for this path, but failing to find it, attempted the hillside.

Weak as I was from loss of blood, I could not keep my seat, and several times slipped off; on the last occasion I was very badly bruised by the stones on which I fell. It appeared to me hopeless to think of getting further. I therefore entreated Pottinger to leave me to my fate, and attend to his own safety. He most nobly and generously refused to do so. He told me to lie quiet and rest myself, while he made search for a path. This he found, and then rested for a while himself. After about an hour's delay, I was remounted, and we succeeded in crossing the mountain, but at the foot of it to our horror found ourselves in an encampment of nomad Afghan shepherds, whose black goat's hair tents we could not see till we were among them. Their dogs barked furiously, but luckily the night was bitterly cold, and no one had the courage to face it.

There were two ways from this camp, we chose one to the right; we hoped by skirting the hike which here lay between us and Kabool, to get into the cantonments at the side furthest from the town, but Pottinger could not find the way, so we were compelled to push on for Deh-Afghana, a large castle in the suburbs of the town of Kabool,

---

26. His statement to the late Sir H. Laurence is appended.

under the walls of which we needs must pass. There were sentries on the towers who challenged us. Pottinger answered in Persian, strongly flavoured with a Milesian accent, that we were the servants of a native chief whom he named. The answer was not quite satisfactory, for the sentry said, "Stop, I'll come down."

Our side replied, "All right," and calculating when our friend had commenced his descent, we pushed on as fast as we could get our horses to go. We got into the town, and in the outskirts dropped our sutler, at the semi-fortified house of one of the Hindoo Shikarporee merchants. He, poor man, to be sure, had had no fighting, but he had been several days without water. He had with him a large bundle of property, which he conveyed into his stronghold. Maun Sing, my orderly, who was also on foot, declined the option of remaining here, and determined to share the remaining danger with us.

We thought of making for the Bala Hissar, where we hoped to be received by the king, but for some reason changed our plan. We passed nearly through the city, meeting only one single person awake, a *fakeer*, smoking his pipe, who gave us his blessing as we passed. We got into the path leading to the cantonment, and were near the end of it, when, to our horror, we found the open shops on either side of the way, which was not twenty feet wide, filled with men. We were called upon to stop, but did not. Then arose a cry of "Stop them," "*Infidels*," etc., etc., followed up by a fusillade which did no injury to anyone but perhaps themselves.

Truly in this, as in so many other instances, Providence protected us, for if any had had the courage to put out his hand and seize our bridles, we had been lost. The fire put a little spirit into our weary animals, who took us clear of them. Maun Sing kept up with us. And here I must correct a mistake into which Pottinger has fallen in his account. He says Maun Sing's accoutrements were hid by a *posteen* or sheep's-skin cloak; this is a mistake, of which I was further assured by Maun Sing himself five or six years afterwards. A man could not possibly have made such a march, still less run for his life, clothed in such a garment. I believe it was Maun Sing's cross belts and breast plate that first disclosed who we were.

Our troubles were not yet at an end. The firing had roused the English garrison, and we were challenged by sentries in a large fort to our right, then in succession by those to our left in the cantonment field work, and we had no small difficulty in passing the jealous and inexorable sentries round two and a half sides of it to the only gate by which we could get access. Here I was taken off my horse, and for the first time had my wounds dressed in the guard-room. *Then* I felt that if it had been to save me from immediate death, I could not have gone ten yards further. We were, to use the words of Eyre, received "as men who had risen from the dead."

Though this is intended to be a personal narrative, I cannot refrain from giving some account of the fate of my comrades. I enjoyed peculiar opportunities of learning particulars from the Afghans themselves during the many months spent in captivity among them; and also from having collected the survivors of the corps in 1842, and conducted them back to India.

It appears then that the doctor, when he went back to the barrack from the parade ground, found that the party which should have joined us, had taken the direct road to Kabool; he joined them and, I presume, failed to induce the men to return. The party was fired upon while passing through the fortified village of Kala Bagh at about 1 a.m. and this we heard. They struggled on till daylight, when they had a fight with the enemy crossing a hill I believe at Ak-Serae, where the man who gave me these particulars was badly wounded with a spear and taken prisoner. All the rest of this party, excepting the doctor, were here either killed, or wounded and taken prisoners.

The doctor, who was mounted, managed to get clear, and by nine or ten o'clock had got nearly to the foot of the last range between Char-ee-kar and Kabool; the range which we crossed next night. Had he succeeded in ascending it, he would have found the pass occupied, but he was not fated to do so. He met some labourers from the town. They surrounded him. He gave one his horse, another his sword,[27] a third his pistols, and in fact diverted himself of all he had, walking on afoot. His horse no doubt had given in. One of the woodcutters followed him, and, to use his own words as communicated to me, felled him with his axe "for the love of God."

Ensign Rose and Sergeant Hanrahan, with those men who adhered to them, as has already been narrated, followed the same track as ourselves, or nearly so, as far as Istalif; they kept to the foot of the

---

27. This sword had belonged to Lieutenant Rattray, killed at Char-ee-kar, regarding which there is a story told by Pottinger, which I saw in one of the English papers in 1843. Rattray bought this sword from the widow of its last owner, who met a violent death. The tradition was that every owner, from the time of Nadir Shah in 1740, had met with a violent death. It was offered to me, being a fine Damascus blade, but I declined to have an article with such an ominous legend attached to it. The doctor in consequence kept it for himself.

western hills, and by morning had gained the Mama Khatoon pass in advance of us, to our right, when they were surrounded and cut up. All accounts I have received, agree in stating that they made a gallant defence,[28] and fought hard for their lives. I think up to the time of the retreat of the army from Kabool, only one, or at the outside two, of the corps had found their way into cantonment; but one man, Motee Ram Havildar, actually found his way past Jellalabad to India.[29]

After General Pollock's advance, I collected 165 men, survivors of the regiment, who were distributed to the Goorkha regiments in India. Maun Sing was honoured and promoted: a love affair, however, got him into difficulty, and he, knowing his countrymen well, fled for his life; but he was befriended by Captain (later General) Troup, whom he had attended as an orderly during the retreat from Kabool. He was enlisted in the 48th N. I., and was engaged in the battles of the first Seik war where he lost his thumb, while orderly to Major George Broadfoot, then Governor-General Agent, who lost his life on that occasion. Maun Sing was pensioned, and had beside the Order of Merit to which a pension was attached. He came all the way from Almorah to Chyabassa, in August 1848, to see me, since when I have not heard of him.

Most of the wounded who were unable to move out from Char-ee-kar with us, were slaughtered next day. It is curious that the enemy either did not discover our retreat, or were afraid to venture near, till long after daylight. We had all throughout the siege sounded our bugles with the regularity of peaceable times, by way of a hint to the enemy that we were all right. On this last fatal morning, the Bugle major, of whose gallantry I have already spoken , and who was too severely wounded to leave with us, crawled up to a bastion and sounded the customary bugle at dawn.

---

28. Forty or fifty were taken prisoners, amongst whom were Oomer Sing, the senior *subadar*, and his wife. The *subadar* of artillery who wounded me, passing the castle where this man was a prisoner, caused him to be put to death, and the poor *subadar's* widow, long a prisoner, used to go daily to weep over his bleaching bones.
29. One of the survivors, I met at Buxa, Bootan (!), January, 1867.

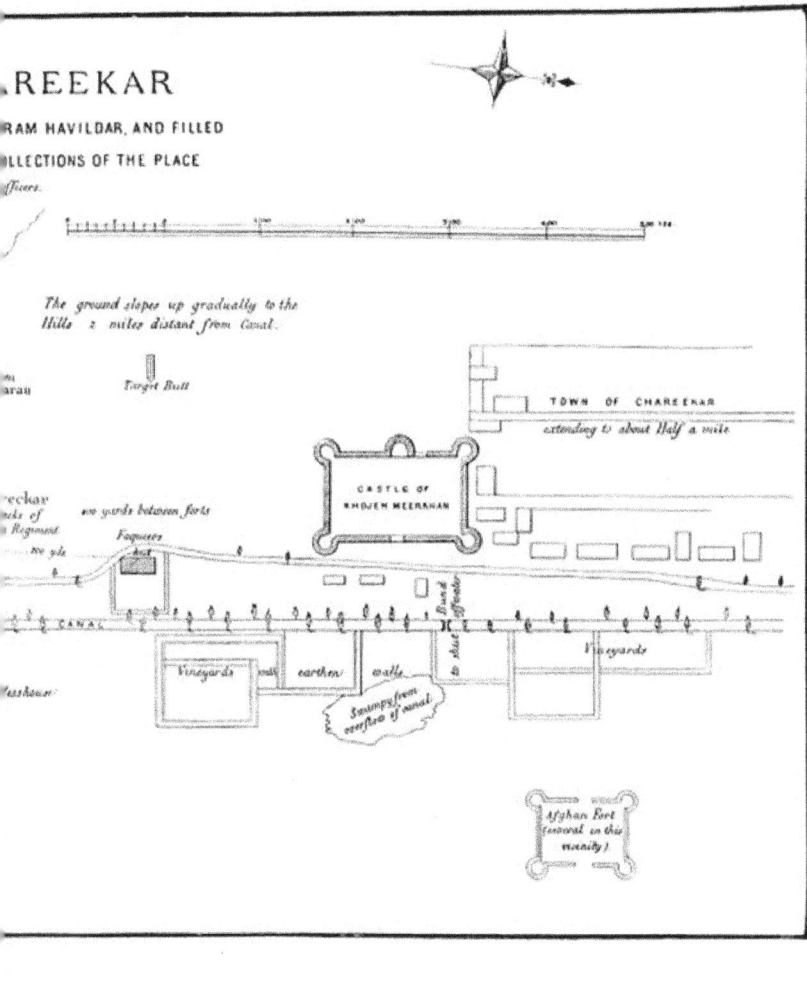

Appendix A

COPY OF LETTER FROM MAJOR ELDRED POTTINGER
TO R. HAUGHTON, ESQ.

> Village of Bynoh Hissar,
> One and a half miles east of Kabool,
> 29th May, 1842.

My dear Mr. Haughton,

I was gratified by your letter of the 26th of February, only a few days received, or should have answered it earlier, for I can assure you, I can most fully sympathize with your anxiety about your gallant son. Your prediction of non-relief from anxiety has long ere this proved true, showing how correctly you viewed our situation.

Your son was cut down in a mutiny of the artillerymen, previous to our evacuation of the fortified barrack of Char-ee-kar, and no language I am master of is sufficient to express my admiration of the fortitude and resolution he showed. It was particularly owing to his example and his exertions, that we were able to hold out as long as we did; and before Captain Codrington, his commanding officer, died, he requested me to make special mention of him to the Government, and to represent to Sir William Macnaghten, that his conduct had shewn him well fitted to command the regiment. The wounds he received, there was not time to dress before we marched, so that he had to bear up against their pain for two nights and a day.

When we left Kabool, he was left behind: the two sword cuts on his shoulder and neck were nearly well, as was that on his left arm, while the stump of the right arm was rapidly improving.

Since my being brought here, I have been unable to see him, but learn by means of the servants that he is quite well again, and I have every hope of seeing him shortly. The first opportunity I have, I shall send him your letter; he expressed much anxiety to send information to you, particularly on Mrs. Haughton's account, and I believe his letters were lost during our unfortunate attempt to retreat. Haughton and I were inmates of the same room from the time we reached camp till Sir William Macnaghten's murder, when I was obliged to leave off care of self. At that period, things were as bad as they could be; the military would neither fight nor fly, and we had neither food nor fuel. I was compelled to renew Sir William Macnaghten's convention by the same causes that he was compelled to open it, and the result, you will ere this have learned, was the utter destruction of the force. I have been preserved by giving myself up as a hostage to ensure the performance of the treaty demands; both parties broke their pledges, and I am of course a prisoner.

The ladies of the party were promised protection by Mahomed Ukbar Khan, and as our army would not protect them, and that Chiefs family were in our hands, I recommended that they should take advantage of his offer, and fortunately they did, for they have been and are well treated, after the manner of the Afghans. General Pollock's force has been at Jelallabad for nearly two months, but he is paralyzed by the arrangements of Sir Jasper Nichols, of the Commissariat department, and want of definite instructions. In return for your prediction, I will also venture my opinion that, if more energy and wisdom are not shown, we shall in all probability receive another check. With General Pollock's army some of the worst officers have been sent.

The most miserable arrangements have been made, particularly in the Commissariat, so that I doubt if Pollock's ability will be able to master it, unless he has the fullest powers and support The service is excessively unpopular with both officers and men; the former are great pecuniary losers, and the latter have been so alienated from their officers by Lord W. Bentinck's arrangements, that they have no longer that care for the service; we no longer get the sons of respectable landholders, but the poor and needy, to keep whom in order, the lash is absolutely necessary, but not to be used, from his wise measure to gain "*Home popularity.*"

Latterly every effort has been made to reduce the power of the commanding officers, and Government has, as you may see here, nearly succeeded. All our old soldiers regret the past times, however, and would rather have the old system than the new. If the Government does not take some decided steps to recover the affections of the army, I really think a single spark will blow the *sepoys* into mutiny: for the zeal of the officers is cold, and it has been that alone which prevents the spirit hitherto. The sole cause of our defeat was not this, to be sure, but it in a great measure aided the incompetence of leaders; but everyone in the force knew with what contempt military suggestions had been received, and that, joined to other causes, rendered them careless of consequences, and I believe many thought the sooner they could get back the better, and hence did not oppose our retreat. Shah Shooja was murdered at the end of February; his son, however, still holds out in the Bala Hissar or citadel, and will be able to do so, I believe, some weeks longer. If Pollock can advance before the Bala Hissar falls, he will not meet much opposition, otherwise I fear he will. Trusting you will excuse this rough scrawl, which is written sitting on the floor, with my knee as a support,

   I remain, my dear Sir,
     Yours very sincerely,
      Eldred Pottinger.

Appendix B

EXTRACT OF A LETTER FROM MAJOR CODRINGTON
TO A FRIEND IN ENGLAND

I wrote to you from Kabool on 28th September, when I was disappointed in my hope of being able to visit the scene of dear Christopher's gallant struggle at Char-ee-kar, but a day or two afterwards a party of horse with Sir E. Shakespere was sent to Char-ee-kar, and I got leave to join him. Henry Lawrence also accompanied us. We started, disguised as Afghans, soon after dusk, and after a fatiguing ride of forty miles reached Char-ee-kar, just as the troops had quitted the ground.

I could only therefore take a hasty glance at the place which poor Christopher defended, and where he found his grave. It does not deserve the name of fort, it is merely a range of *sepoy'* huts forming a square enclosure, the outer wall not being high enough above the roof to form a parapet. There was a broad gate- way, but no gate; and opposite the small house which the officers occupied; you may conceive the difficulty of defending such a place even under favourable circumstances; but besides the defects I have mentioned, it was commanded on one side by a more lofty fort from which the party which first occupied it were drawn, the other side by rising ground.

A sort of parapet was made by tearing up the tents and making tand bags: but the soil being full of pebbled, in fact composed almost entirely of them, they were scattered about when struck by a ball, and did more harm than good; not a drop of water was to be had, except when the garrison sallied forth and fought for it; and how the place was held for a fortnight against overpowering numbers, is scarcely conceivable. The bravery of the garrison must have been beyond all praise, and their exertions unremitting.

In the centre of the enclosure stood the magazine, in which dear Christopher and Lieutenant Salusbury were buried in one grave; it was a mass of ruins, the walls and roof destroyed, and the exact spot undistinguishable among the mass of rubbish. I could only stay for a minute, but it was a melancholy satisfaction to stand on the spot which had been hallowed by the presence of one so dear to me, and to pay the tribute of affection over his grave. I was obliged to hurry off, to overtake the rear guard of the troops, and after a ride of ten miles further reached the new ground, thoroughly knocked up.

Appendix C

STATEMENT OF PUDDUM SING, FIRST OF SHAH SHOOJA'S 4TH OR GHOORKA REGIMENT, 8TH COMPANY, THEN OF THE 8TH COMPANY NUSSEREE BATTALION, AND NOW *HAVILDAR* IN THE 8TH COMPANY 1ST GOORHKA REGIMENT—A NATIVE OF PALEE PACHOUNG CHOWKOTE PUTTI, WEST OF ALMORAH, MADE AT BUXA, BHOOTAN, JANUARY 12TH, 1867.

I was left wounded and unable to move on the evacuation of Char-ee-kar; we remained all night, expecting to be murdered. Next morning the Affghans came and stripped us of our clothing. Some were killed. Heera Sing was *subadar* of my Company, he was wounded in a night attack at 8 p. m. It was 8 p. m. when the troops evacuated Char-ee-kar. I remained at Char-ee-kar with the *subadar* till he went into Cabul, (that is the *subadar* who surrendered his post); he was a Kankee, his name was ——— Adhikaree. I lay for nine months wounded at Char-ee-kar.

A *bunniah* took me to Kalabagh, whence we fled on the advance of the troops. I met Lieutenant McKean of the Khelat-i-Ghilzee Regiment between Ghuznee and Kandahar. He, on hearing that I was of the 4th Regiment, questioned me and put me through my facings; being satisfied, he took me to Captain Craigie, by whose orders I was enlisted in the regiment.

When we got to Cabul, I wished to join the survivors of my own corps, but was told that all regiments were the same, and that I must remain where I was. When we were encamped near Seeah Sung, I went and made my *salam* to you.

I was with the party who first went to the relief of Major Pottinger's fort at Lugmanee. The 7th and 8th companies went, and the same companies were sent there again the next day, and also were engaged in the first fight at Char-ee-kar. I do not distinctly remember the commencement of the outbreak, but so much that one day it was reported Mr. Rattray was killed, then the two companies were sent out. We had two men wounded, the enemy had seven or eight killed, I bayoneted one myself. I do not know the actual loss on one side or the other. That same night Mohun Beer Moonshee, Major Pottinger and a Keranee Sahib came to our place, it may have been the next night; the morning after they came, I heard from an old *sepoy* of my Company that the enemy had got into their fort. So our men escaped by a postern gate. I do remember that some of our men remained on sentry at the towers at Lugmanee after the rest came away.

I was in the fight which took place at the corner of the Charee-kar *bazar*. We drove the enemy out of their first shelter, and we took cover in the canal, from which the enemy had suffered the water to escape; from thence our *sepoys* began to advance one or two at a time; you called out to them not to advance, as the enemy were too many for us. I remember you wrote on a piece of paper with charcoal to Captain Codrington for more men and for what else I don't know. We went on after that.

I was with Captain Codrington when he was wounded in our *bazar*, the people of which had gone inside the barrack; he was wounded in the breast; I do not remember when Major Pottinger was wounded.

I was wounded the night when Ensign Rose went out with two or three companies. Heramunee Soobadar and three or four of our men were killed. We passed out by the parade ground and through the enemy's entrenchments, when Ensign Rose fired. I was then wounded in the right thigh and left arm, and became unconscious. I remained in hospital for eight or nine days previous to the retreat.

I heard you were wounded by a Golundaz. I was lying in great pain with the wound in my leg at the time, but struggled to the door, and saw you returning towards the hospital. People said to the *sepoys* who were with you, "Why did you not prevent this?"

A *havildar* said, "Who should know that we had an enemy within? we were watching the enemy without."

I remained with Jye Deb Brahmin, and an Eastern man whose name I don't know, for nine months, at the ash pit of Hummam (Turkish bath), for the sake of its warmth. Jye Deb was in the battalion at Kangra, and died there.

I think there were about one hundred men left wounded or

dying in hospital. Some were killed, some were carried away, some went with Soubadar ——— Adhikari; the man lying next to me was killed, because he did not get up quick enough. I received a thrust of a bayonet. A *sepoy* came to the Hospital and said, the *soubadar* called us. I went towards the town, but never saw him. An Akhoon fed me; after my wound healed, the limb remained stiff; he told me to rub it daily with ghee in the sun, and I should be able to use it. I did so, and was able to move about.

I heard that the English had taken the Khyber Pass: when I saw the people fleeing, with their families, I knew it to be true. We heard that the Burra[1] Sahibs had been taken away to Bameean, and that Akber Kan intended to keep them till his father[2] was released. I once heard Afghans say that they had lost at Char-ee-kar and Cabul from two thousand to two thousand five hundred men. I don't know what chiefs were killed.

I don't know when Captain Codrington died, or where he was buried. I believe he died the night after he was wounded, but it was kept secret, for fear the men should be dispirited. We were told you said he was alive, and that relief was coming from Cabul. There were four of us in the Khelat-i-Ghilzie Regiment, *viz* Hunnooman Doobay, Natoo Sonar. Dhurmoo and myself; in the 3rd Hill regiment five, and seven entered the Hill regiment of Pheroo (Ferris?) Saheb.

I heard that when the troops left Char-ee-kar, some went with you some in another direction, and others with Mr. Rose followed you. I heard that he and Hunnooman Jemadar were killed. Jye Deb's wife was with him, she was young; we were often threatened in joke, but no one interfered with us. I don't know who was the owner of the fort near us; it was a musket shot and a half distant from us. I don't know what became of the ——— Adhikari. Jye Deb once went to the barracks, he told me there was nothing there but men's skulls and bones.

The stream in front of our barracks, was half a musket shot distant, I was[3] fifteen or sixteen days without any water at all. The only food I had after I was wounded, was once some raw mutton and a *seer* of coarse flour which I had by me; part of it I ate dry. I believe there were about 200 killed and wounded before the retreat. Mohun Beer is in a *ressaleh* at Kohat.

---

1. The English officers.
2. Ameer Dost Mahomed Khan.
3. This statement I have no doubt was made in perfect good faith, we all had lost count of time.

Statement of Bullay Sarkie, Naik, 1st Goorkha Regiment, 6th Company, Made at Buxa, Bhootan, 13th January, 1867.

When about twelve years of age. I was at Cabul with my sister's husband, Sookea Sarkie, *havildar* of Shah Schooja's 4th or Ghoorka Regiment, 6th Company. I went with the regiment by way of Shikarpore in 1838. I was with the regiment at Bameean, Syghan, and at Char-ee-kar.

The night we retreated from that place, I left by the postern gate with my sister's husband and his companions, I was with you.

The 1st, 2nd, 3rd and 4th Companies were formed into a square, and the women and children were placed in the centre; in this manner we started. We soon, however, broke up and were scattered about. At daylight we reached Khoja Serai; there were: about 250 men and 16 women. At between 7 and 8 o'clock fighting began. Mr. Rose, and the quarter master, Sergeant Hanrahan, and the *soubadar* of the 2nd Company were killed. They killed some of the women and seized me and the rest. I remained eleven months in a Shikarpore Khutree's[4] house. When troops came, I joined them and met you.

You gave me four *rupees* for expenses. I came to India with Nowell Sing, attached to Broadfoot's Sappers. Seven or eight hundred of the enemy surrounded us at Khoja Serai. Only three or four of our party escaped. About fifty were collected from different quarters, and kept at Khoja Serai for two and a half months, then Prince Futteh Jung sent for them, saying he would employ them. The Hindoo shopkeepers had supported them up to that time. They all eventually came to you and served with Broadfoot's Sappers.

I myself saw Mr. Rose killed; they called upon him to lay down his arms; he threw down his pistol, whereon they shot him, and afterwards hacked him with their long knives. The quarter master sergeant was cut down with their knives, the bodies remained where they fell. Mr. Rose's dog stayed by his body for ten days; I often called it, but it would not come away. I do not know what became of it, none of the bodies were buried.

The fight lasted about an hour; the spot where Mr. Rose was killed was about two miles on the Cabul side of Khoja Serai.

---

4. Hindoo merchant of Shikarpore, in Sind.

Our men did not make any stand, they were killed in flight. Many of the survivors of the Corps are in the Sappers and Miners at Huftabad (Abbotabad?) The fight lasted fifteen days at Char-ee-kar.

Appendix D

Extract from the *Englishman* Newspaper, of Calcutta April 27th, 1842.

Personal narrative of Havildar Motee Ram, of the Shah's 4th or Ghoorkha Regiment of Light Infantry, destroyed at Char-ee-kar

The 4th Regiment was sent to Char-ee-kar in the month of May. We were placed in garrison in the *guree*, then in progress of erection. Major Pottinger and some other gentlemen were in another *guree*, distant about a *coss* from ours, and called Kalla Lukman.[1] To this latter fort we furnished a party of 100 men, under a *soubadar*—this party was relieved weekly. The *guree* of Char-ee-kar in which we were placed was quadrangular in figure, 100 yards long in each face, and having a bastion at each angle—the ditch from which the earth had been excavated to build up the walls, at the deepest was only three feet, in other parts not more than two feet deep.

A *Khutria*, named Hur Singh, was engaged in building the *guree* by contract. The *guree* of Char-ee-kar is marked A in the accompanying sketch; there were two gateways to it, with gates, one to the west, another to the east, marked 1 and 2 in the sketch. At 2 was the quarter guard of the regiment, at 1 its rear guard; outside of the gate No. 2 was a number of huts inhabited by the *bazar* people of the 4th Regiment; in this gateway was placed a long and heavy native gun, I should think an eighteen-pounder; on[2] each of the two bastions marked 3 and 4 was placed one of the *Shah's* six-pounders.

---
1. Killa Lughmanee.
2. The bastion nearest the town alone had a gun.—J. C. H.

A small thread of water was conducted from the neighbouring hills, and a hollow formed from working up the earth with water to raise the walls of the *guree*; after the flow of water into this hollow was stopped by the Afghans, there continued stagnant in it about fifteen *mussucks*, *vide* No. 5. There were no guns on the bastions marked 6 and 7. I have shown how all the artillery we had—the three guns already mentioned—were disposed of. The huts for the *sepoys* were arranged along the interior sides of the *guree*, connected together and flat-roofed. There is no water within the fort of Char-ee-kar, which stands on a plain, no hills approaching it nearer than four miles. Our officers' quarters were at the westward gate. In front of the eastern face of Char-ee-kar, and distant from its walls 150 feet, ran a canal B B B, with shelving banks 20 feet in breadth at the top, and about 15 feet deep.

The water which ran in it was generally waist deep; this canal was fed by a river to the north, and about six miles distant from Char-ee-kar—the road to Lughman crossed[3] the canal on which there is a bridge the road is marked 8 8 8 8, and to prevent injury to the cultivation, was made to wind considerably to the N..E. of bastion No. 3. About 26 yards off was situated a *fakhir's* hut and *tukeah*,—this is marked C in the sketch. To the south of bastion No. 4, distant also some 200 yards, there was an extensive vineyard D; about the same distance, there stood to the S.W. of bastion No. 7 a *Musjeed* marked E.

At F were three tombs of European officers, nearly, I should say, 400 yards from bastion No. 6. G was the target practice butt, distant from, and north of the same bastion, 350 yards. H was a small *guree* behind the *fakhir's* hut, and 500 yards from the fort of Char-ee-kar. The site of the town of Char-ee-kar is marked I I, while K denotes that of the fort of Lughman.

A few days before the Dewallee, Mr. Rattray, who commanded one of the Affghan corps, was lured out from the fort of Lughman by Shah Mahommed of Nijrow, to look, he said, at some recruits which he brought with him for service. They were mounted men. As Lt. Rattray was examining them drawn up in a line. Shah Mahommed gave his troopers a wink, when they

---

3. There is some confusion of ideas here; the road from Char-ee-kar and Lughmanee ran parallel to the canal for about three miles, then crossed the canal at right angles to the castle, distant about 500 yards.—J. C. H.

wheeled up from the right and left, and enclosed Mr. Rattray, who was shot with a pistol, and his body, which was afterwards recovered, hacked to pieces. I heard this from the Goorkha Moonshee Mohun Beer who accompanied Mr. Rattray, but escaped under the horses' bellies.

The men who murdered Mr. Rattray now made a dash at the fort of Lughman. Mr. Rattray's regiment[4] of Affghans immediately joined the assailants. The attack had continued for the space of two hours, the Affghans being kept at bay by our guard. Capt. Codringrton then directed[5] Lieut. Haughton to take the 2nd and 8th Companies to reinforce Lughman. Our men took each 60 rounds of ammunition in their pouches. When they had expended 50 in skirmishing, and killing numbers of the Affghans, they were ordered to close and charge; they did so; a great number of the Affghans sought refuge in a vineyard, but were almost entirely destroyed by the bayonet and *cookry*.[6] All the Affghans who had been attacking the fort of Lughman drew off, and our two companies returned to that of Char-ee-kar, which they reached at 3 o'clock p.m.[7] A few hours afterwards firing was heard at Lughman—the Affghans were fired upon by our people when endeavouring to remove their head.

The following morning it was observed that the enemy were very numerous about Lughman, and pressing its garrison hard; so[8] at 6 a.m. the 1st, 3rd, and 6th companies of my regiment, with a six-pounder drawn by bullocks, under the command of Lieutenant Haughton, issued from the Ghurree Char-ee-kar, with the view of assisting our troops at Lughman. We advanced, until we arrived within half a mile of Lughman, without opposition; at this point a body of 1,000 of the enemy's infantry, with a few horsemen interspersed amongst them, attempted to cut off our way; this party we easily repulsed. We now had arrived at a bridge near Lughman, on (at) which our six-pounder was placed; suddenly from all quarters a rush was made for the gun

---

4. There were only a few horsemen with the Political Agent.—J. C. H.
5. It will be seen from my narrative that Motee Ram is mistaken, Captain Codringston being himself shut up in Lughmanee.—J. C. H.
6. The *cookry* is a Goorkha weapon.
7. This is also a mistake; they did not get back till dark.—J. C. H.
8. It will be seen from my narrative that Motee Ram was ignorant of the cause for which this party was sent out, and his memory is at fault as to some details.—J. C. H.

by immense multitudes of Affghans, who had concealed themselves in the vineyards and different buildings round about.

It is difficult to form any accurate notion of the number of our assailants so scattered, but it struck me there must have been 25,000—all the villages of Kohistan, Punjsheer, and Gorband poured forth their inhabitants against us; the whole male population in this quarter of Affghanistan had taken the *Ghazi's* oath.

Our front, rear, and both flanks were attacked simultaneously, but the most serious attack was in front, or from the Lughman side, the plain between which and where we were was completely crowded with Affghans. We repulsed them all with great slaughter, but suffered severe loss ourselves. Lieutenant Salusbury[9] was killed—shot in the chest, and placed in one of the two *doolies* we had with us. The quarter master sergeant was wounded. The *soubadar* of my company, the 6th, Singh Beer by name, and a most gallant officer, was put in the second *doolie*. The quarter master sergeant was able to walk, supported by two *sepoys*.

We had now been absent three hours from the *guree* of Char-ee-kar, a great part of which time we were seriously engaged. It was now observed that heavy bodies of the enemy were against Char-ee-kar itself. We were ordered to retrace our steps; the 1st company was thrown out as skirmishers to cover our retreat; those badly wounded it was impossible to carry off with us, we were so hotly assailed. The Affghans quickly killed them, and seemed to take much delight in mutilating their dead bodies, and pitching their severed members to a distance from each other.[10] We fought our way back to the *gurree* of Char-ee-kar, which we reached about 10 o'clock a.m.

The Affghans now surrounding the fort of Char-ee-kar, and seeking shelter from our fire behind the walls of the vineyard, the target practice butt, officers' tombs, *musjeed* and *fakhir's* hut, annoyed us very much; it rained bullets. Leaving 200 men in the fort, and taking out the two six-pounders, Captain Codrington drove the enemy from all the positions they had taken

---

9. The sergeant was wounded in the chest, and sent in on the only *dooly* we had; Salusbury, mortally wounded, walked half a mile to the barracks, supported by two men. We had but one *dooly*.—J. C. H.
10. This is a pure piece of imagination.—J. C. H.

up around us. At the second discharge one of the six-pounders[11] broke down. The Affghans entirely vanished for the present, but the water ceased to run in the canal B B B. We found afterwards that the Affghans had diverted it to the eastward at the point marked L. Our casualties in the whole of this day were very numerous. About 10 o'clock p.m. when the canal had become dry, the enemy appeared again, retaking possession of all their former positions and of the now dry canal besides, the banks of which effectually screened them from our fire.

Towards morning the attack on the fort became more feeble, until at last it ceased altogether; however about 7 o'clock the whole mass of the enemy precipitated itself against the fort; horse and foot leaguered us round on every side. The two six-pounders (we had mended the broken one in the course of the night) were taken out with the greater part of the regiment, while the long gun fired from the gateway on the enemy. One of the six-pounders again broke down; the bulk of the enemy were again beaten off, but a continued skirmishing amongst the vineyards and different buildings was kept up until nightfall: half the men of the regiment remained in the fort, while half skirmished, and thus relieved each other alternately.

At 10 o'clock p. m. Major Pottinger, another gentleman, and the party from Lughman which had been as busy as ourselves, joined us. The want of water began to be felt severely by us; there was scarcely any provision within the fort. We did not mind that so much as the torments of thirst. The enemy continued attacking us daily. On the 3rd day, as well as I can remember, all the Affghans collected in a body to capture the long gun at the gateway; there were whole *beeghas* of gleaming swords moving towards us, and shouts of a "*Chari yar. Alli Mudut*" rent the air. We answered them back at every discharge of the long gun, "*Gorucknath kejy.*" This assault was by far the most severe we had yet experienced. Major Pottinger and the other European officers said they never witnessed such a conflict.

Capt. Codrington was shot through the chest. He was carried to his quarters alive, but died shortly after. Major Pottinger was wounded in the thigh. We charged the Affghans and drove them in the direction of the point were the water was turned off. On

---

11. This too is incorrect; the gun broke down while I was firing it, on our retreat. J.C. H.

this occasion we partially destroyed the *Fakhir's Tukea* where we always observed the Affghans clustered thickest. Next day, a seer of water was served out to each man by Lieut. Haughton; this water was obtained from the hollow marked 5 in the sketch. The second day after, half a *seer* was supplied; in a few days it diminished to a *chittack*, and at last ceased altogether.

Some *doombahs* [sheep] were given to us by the officers; we found relief from sucking the raw flesh, and some of the men placed the contents of the stomach of the sheep in cloths, and wringing them very hard obtained some moisture to assuage their raging thirst. The sick and wounded now increased to a frightful amount, and were continually screaming for water in piercing accents. Our muskets were so foul from incessant use that the balls were forced down with difficulty, although separated from the paper of the cartridge which usually wraps them round. The lips of the men became swollen and bloody, and their tongues clove to their palates.

I ought to have mentioned that the day Capt. Codrington was killed, your old Shikarree[12] at Lohooghat, Nur Singh, was also slain. He was the best shot among us; every time he fired he killed an Affghan. The European officers were so pleased with him, that he was to have been made a *jemader*. Days and nights rolled on. We were continually engaged with the enemy; the men used to steal out in the night to the spring which formerly supplied the hollow marked 5, but which the Affghans turned off in another direction. Those who had the canteens you sent up with the last Goorkha's levies, used them; those who had *lotas* only, took them with them covered in clothes, lest the glitter of the metal should lead to detection; those who had neither *lotas* nor canteens resorted to the use of cloths which they dipped in the fountain and brought back saturated with moisture.

When any of these adventurous spirits returned to the fort, all struggled round them to procure one precious drop. The Affghans, however, found out the practice, and shot down all those who approached the spring. For two days there was not a single drop of water within the wall of the fort; the men were mad with thirst, and demanded to be led against any perils to pro-

---

12. "Your old Shikaree" Motee Ram was addressing this narrative to Major McSherry personally.—Ed. *Englishman*.

cure water. Accordingly, at midnight, Lieut. Rose[13] conducted a party of 100 men, taking with them all the *lotas* and canteens they could carry, and all the *bhistees* and non-combatants to the spot marked M, where the water from the new cut had overflowed its banks, by the route marked by arrows pointing from the Gurree of Char-ee-kar.

Having luxuriated for a short time in the delicious element, and filled our vessels with it, Lieut. Rose took us to a field of radishes marked N. Here we crammed as many as we could into our mouths and stuck our belts full of more for our comrades in the fort, to which we set out on our return by the route indicated by arrows pointing towards it. Shah Mahomed with a body of 3,000 men had taken post at the spot marked O at an early hour of the night, and erected his standard at P.—A great number of his men were in the now dry bed of the canal B B B.; they seemed to keep a negligent look out.

Lieut. Rose said to us, "Give them one volley, then the steel you know to use so well." The non-combatants carrying the water were placed out of harm's way behind a wall. We fired together by word of command from Lieutenant Rose on the slumbering crowd of faces within 50 yards of them. We then charged shouting "*Goruknath ke-jy*," and set the bayonet and *cookry* to work with a will. A company drawn up in readiness at the gateway to assist us, should we require their aid, heard our battle-cry, rushed down to the canal B B B. extended itself along its banks on the Char-ee-kar fort side, and slew the Afghans as they tried to scramble out on that side.

On the opposite we were performing the same operations. Those who had *cookries* did most execution; there is no weapon like the *cookry* for a hand-to-hand fight. Mahomed Shah himself was killed, and we captured his green flag, and carried it off in triumph to the Fort Char-ee-kar. Shah Mahomed's flag was a very magnificent one; its staff was surmounted by a trident [crescent?] and ball of gold, and the flag itself was six feet long and equally broad, made of the finest green broadcloth, with a figure of the sun splendidly embroidered in the centre. It was an old acquaintance of ours, and changed bearers frequently, as we successively shot them during our long term of fighting. We had somewhat spoiled its beauty too, by piercing it with bullets;

---

13. Ensign A. Rose, 54th N. I.—Ed.

the artificial sun shining in the light of the real one, as it waved out in the breeze, offered a famous mark.

We were as happy in Char-ee-kar that night as we could be under the heavy loss of our fallen comrades, and in sight of the sufferings of those wounded, who were stretched on the ground thickly around us. The thirst of all[14] was completely relieved, and their hunger partially so. Our officers were proud of us, and we were proud of ourselves and of each other. The officers said, Shah Mahomed's flag should be ever retained in the regiment as a memorial of that night's achievement. For some days after the capture of Shah Mahomed's flag, and the death of its owner, the enemy relaxed his efforts and we our fire. This interval of comparative repose was most grateful and refreshing to us.

The number of Afghans had very perceptibly diminished in our vicinity. Five days[15] passed when the horrors of thirst began to assail us again. At last a message was received from the treacherous inhabitants of the town of Char-ee-kar that they dared not turn the water down to us themselves, as they would assuredly be murdered, if they did so; but that we might come and throw a dam across the new cut at L., remove the other dam, and cause the water to flow in its wonted channel again. Two hundred men,[16] accompanied by Lieutenants Haughton and Rose, and taking our *fourahs* or digging tools with us, proceeded along the banks of the canal B B B to L. On the road we had some skirmishing, but not much. As soon as the men came in sight of the water at L, many of them rushed madly forward, and began to drink; while in the act of doing so, a heavy fire was suddenly opened upon them by the ambushed Afghans in the gardens, houses, and behind the walls of the town of Char-ee-kar—this fire caused great havoc amongst us, and we were forced to retreat without effecting our object.

Dying of thirst, lamentably reduced in numbers—weakened by toil and hunger, the Afghans clung more closely round as our exertions in our own defence became less energetic. A mine,[17]

---

14. That is, all of Motee Ram's party.—J. C. H.
15. There is here such complete confusion of ideas as to time, that I feel it impossible to put the narrative right.—J. C. H. 16. This is a mistake, as there were only two digging hoes and two picks with the regiment.—J. C. H.
17. Such a mine was an impossibility; see my account.—J. C. H.

the shaft of which commencing at the *Fukhir's Tukeah* C, and passing by Bastion 3, terminated in a chamber at Bastion 4, was sprung. A third of the Bastion 4 was destroyed, two men were buried in its ruins—the dotted line from C to Bastion No 4 shows the course of the shaft of the mine. The Afghans are very expert miners—they learn the art from continually digging "*Careezes.*"

The explosion of the mine in question seemed to be the signal for another determined onset on the part of the Afghans. The stock of grape shot originally brought from Cabul had been expended, bags were filled with musket balls, and loaded with these; the heavy gun at each discharge cut long lanes in the throng of Mongelas, while we kept up a continual fire from the roofs of the Barracks. The Mussulmans pressed on nevertheless; the party protecting the gun below was annihilated, and the cannon almost in the clutches of the enemy, when Lieutenant Haughton called out, "Down from the walls, every man of you, and rally round the gun, which is nearly in the hands of the enemy, and with it go the lives and honour of us all."

We every one of us rushed out of the gateway, and charged the enemy, who recoiled from the shock as far as the canal B B B, to which they confined themselves, keeping up a dropping fire on the walls of the *gurree*. We buried this day within the fort the bodies of Capt. Codrington, L.Salusbury, the sergeant major, and upwards of 200 of the *sepoys* of the 4th Regiment. The following day the Lohar Mistree[18] of the 4th Regiment, who was a native of Hindoostan, and who served in the regiment from the time it was first raised, but was a Mussulman and married to an Afghan, wife of Char-ee-kar, together with the gunners, who were all Mussulmans from the Punjaub, plotted to leave us, and go over to the enemy. In attempting to put this into execution, they proceeded to the gateway, but as they were going out, Lieut. Haughton seized the *jemadar* of the Golandauze to detain him; the latter immediately drew his sword, cut at Lieut. Haughton, and wounded him in the hand severely, and breaking loose, Lieut. Haughton called out, "Shoot these *nimuck harams.*—they are off to the enemy."

We fired at the party as they ran in the direction of the canal,

---

18. This man was faithful, and gave me his opinion that the gunners were plotting. —J. C. H.

and dropped five of them. The third day[19] after this event, our number brought down to a little more than 200 men fit for action, without water, without foot, and only thirty rounds of ammunition per man remaining, it was determined to evacuate the Gurree of Char-ee-kar, and endeavour to fight our way to Cabul. At midnight we moved out; we had only two *doolies*[20] in which were placed Major Pottinger and Lieut. Haughton, the bearers of all the others were either killed or had died. Nearly 300 of our comrades, dead, dying, or so badly wounded as to be unable to walk, were left behind within the Ghurree of Char-ee-kar. I don't know whether the guns, which were also left behind, were spiked or not.

I think from the death of Lieut. Rattray until the period of our finally evacuating the Gurree of Char-ee-kar, twenty-one or twenty-three days must have elapsed. I had too much to do to take account of time. I cannot give dates, but I narrate events in their order of succession, to the best of my memory. I ought to mention that the walls of the Gurree of Char-ee-kar had only reached the height of one cubit above the roof of the *sepoys'* barracks when the fighting began; consequently so low a parapet gave us little protection from the enemy's *jazails*, which told on us from a distance, one half of which only muskets could carry to with effect. The day after Capt. Codrington's death, to remedy this defect, the officers tore up their tents, and made bags of the canvas, filled them with earth, and placed them on the walls, to cover us from the Afghans' fire.

At the time hostilities broke out, there were two Goorkha *Fakhirs* in the fort, who were visiting on a pilgrimage the different Hindoo shrines in Afghanistan. They demanded that arms and ammunition should be given to them. Our officers complied with their request, and these sturdy and holy personages astonished us all by their feats in action: there were none of us who fought the Afghans better than they did. We marched on during the night without molestation, until we arrived at a village near Kara Bagh, the second regular marching stage from Caubul on the Char-ee-kar road.

Here opposition commenced, and we advanced skirmishing

---

19. Here again Motee Ram is mistaken; it will be seen that the retreat took place the very night I was wounded.—J. C. H.
20. There were no *doolies*; we rode.—J. C. H.

until we reached Kara Bagh, about 3 o'clock a. m. by which time our movements became generally known, and our enemies were getting round us in hopeless numbers every minute. The road ran though the middle of the town of Kara Bagh with walls and vineyards on either side: these the Afghans lined, and from them poured a deadly and frequent fire on us. Numbers were killed—we were totally vanquished; there was a gateway into a vineyard on one side of the road. I rushed through it; an Afghan laid hold of my clothes to detain me, but I shook him off and continued my flight, taking care to carry off my musket with me, for which I had only five rounds remaining in my pouch.

I ascended the summit of the hills, and ensconced myself in a hollow far up in the mountain, where there was water, during the day—on the coming of night, I endeavoured to make my way to Caubul; I had arrived within two miles of the British Cantonments there—when the dawn discovered to me that I had got into the middle of the Afghan troops besieging the place at the time.

I saw at once all hope of further escape was gone. I had 100 *rupees* in my *cummerbund*, which sum I amassed in the *Shah's* service. I took it out and buried it, placing a stone which I thought I could again recognize, over it, and sat down quietly to await what might happen. Shortly a party of horse, about 25 in number, belonging to Hajiz Khan and Bahahdeen approached the spot were I was, and they immediately dismounted—some seized me by the feet, some by the shoulders; one man, taking up my own musket, snapped it three times at me. I am a Mussalman, said I; God does not will that you should kill me—the musket won't go off.

The fatalist I addressed threw down the musket, drew his sabre, and with its sharp edge pressing on my throat called on me to say the *kalma*, else he would immediately sacrifice me. I did repeat the *kalma*—the sabre was removed from my throat and they carried me to Bahahdeen, first depriving me of my coat, pantaloons, a silk handkerchief, a pistol, my shoes and some other articles, leaving me only a pair of *pyjamahs*. Bahahdeen Gurree is situated I should think about three *coss* from the city of Cabul. While I remained with Bahahdeen for five days, the people of the village continually threatened to put me to death.

Bahahdeen at length released me, giving me an old tattered *loonghee* for a turban and my own *chogah*, and saw me a *coss* on my road.

After he left me I had proceeded a *coss*, when a man ploughing on the roadside seized me, and threatened to kill me, unless I worked his plough. I did so until evening, when he took me to his house and there gave me a scanty meal. This man employed me ten days in guiding his plough. While with him, I suffered severely during the night time—the weather was bitter cold, and I had nothing to cover me but my *chogah*, I examined the roof of the house during the day, and it appeared to me that by removing a few of the bricks from a sort of chimney I might get out unobserved. At night I did so, and effected my escape for the time.

I had got five *coss* further on the road to Jellalabad, when the son of a *sirdar* who was fighting at Cabul (I don't know his name), sent some horsemen to take and bring me to him. I was taken to the *gurree*, all the inmates of which, young and old, male and female, gathered round, exclaiming, "A *Kaffir* or *Feringhee*: kill him; kill him;" but the young chief protected me from violence, and told me to groom his horse. This young man was continually looking in the direction of Cabul, through a telescope which he said Sir A. Burnes had given his father as a present. I was hard-worked and ill-fed in this family.

I remained with them about eight days, when the young chief transferred me to a native of Ghorbund who came to his village, and rented his grazing ground for a large flock of camels. I was employed tending these camels for some twenty days. I was not well fed. I had made acquaintance with a servant of my compulsory master. This servant was a Huzara, who received one *rupee* two *annas* a month as wages. He became kindly disposed to me, and one day told me that our master designed to sell me to some Bokhara merchants, with whom he was at that moment driving a bargain about me.

I immediately ran away, to escape the intended sale. On crossing the river at Bhoothak, five Affghans seized me, and asked me if I were a *Feringhee*. I replied in the negative, and stated that I was a discharged camel man of Shah Shooja's; they asked me why Shah Shooja had discharged me. I answered that the King, being mewed up in the Balla Hassar, said he had no employment for camel men at present. Fakeera, my new captor, took me to his house, where I remained some time, hard-worked and ill-fed, as usual. While tending Fakeera's *dhoombahs* in the jungles, I heard a youth say, "Ukhbar has allowed the *Feringhees* to depart today, and our people are following them from Cabul."

When night came on I went to the spot where I had deposited my *rupees*, and regained possession of them. I set off after the British force, and overtook it at Khoord Cabul, as it was setting out from thence. At Jugdulluck the British force was girded round by Ukhbar Khan's horsemen, who were killing all they could. I extricated myself from this scene of carnage, and sought safety once more in the hill tops. I remained a day high up in the hills. I had tasted no food for twenty-six hours from the time I made my last insufficient meal. I was benumbed by the cold, I could no longer contend with the never-ending dangers and hardships which beset me.

I wished for death to release me from sufferings now become intolerable. I descended to the roadside, determined to declare myself to the first Affghans who approached, and court the blow of some pitying sword. I saw a party approach, and concluded the hour of my death had arrived. The party turned out to be five Hindoo *cutries*; these *cutries* said, "As you are a Hindoo, we will save your life you must pay us for doing so, and to make sure of it we will exact payment beforehand."

They then searched me and took the 100 *rupees* out of my *cummerbund*, and returned me ten of them—they conducted me to a *Dhurmsalah* in which there was a Hindoo *fakhir*. His protection I also sought, and gave him my remaining ten *rupees*. He dressed me up in the red dress of a *fakhir*, and rubbed wood ashes over my face. I was to pass for his *chela*, or disciple; and he said I was to accompany him in the character of such on a pilgrimage he proposed making to Hurdwar.

A party of fruit merchants shortly after arrived. The *fakhir*, the *cutries*, and myself joined them. We descended the high road considerably to the left of Peshawar. I begged my way, until I got to Sir Jasper Nicoll's camp, one march this side of Loodianah. The sketch I have drawn shows pretty correctly, I am convinced, Char-ee-kar and all it embraces—you had taught me how to make such sketches. You have known me many years, and you know if I ever told you a lie or brought you false infor-

mation. You will therefore attach such credit to my tale as your appreciation of my character, so familiar to you, may adjudge.
(True translation.)
T. MacSherry, Major, 30th N. I.,
Late Goorkha Recruiting Officer, S. S. F.
Simla, March 31st, 1842.

Appendix E

NARRATIVE OF MOHUN BEER, A MOONSHEE IN THE EMPLOY OF MAJOR ELDRED POTTINGER, CB. THE ORIGINAL STATEMENT, CORRECTED BY SIR R. SHAKESPEAR.

The city of Char-ee-kar in Kohistan is about 46 miles direct north of Cabool. In November, 1841, there was a cantonment about half a mile north of the city, in which was stationed the 4th Regiment of Shah Shoojah's Infantry (742 strong) and three of H M.'s. guns, which with their men had been in the service of Dost Mahomed Khan.

The officers present with the regiment were Captain Codrington, commanding; Lieut. Haughton, Adjutant, Lieut. Salusbury, quarter master; and Ensign Rose; there was also a sergeant major by name Burns, and a quarter master sergeant named Hanrahan. The fort of Lughmani is about one and a half miles from the cantonments, and in it resided at the time now alluded to Major E Pottinger, C. B., Political Agent: Lieut. Rattray, Asst. Political Agent, and Mr. Asst. Surgeon. The fort was a square of about 50 paces,[1] the walls of mud of considerable thickness and about 60[2] feet high.

The cantonment was dependent for its supply of water on a water course; and the destruction of this small force by the Kohistanees appears to have been mainly caused by their having turned off the stream into another channel.

On the morning of 3rd November, 1841, about 9 o'clock, I saw about 3,000 Kohistanees collected round the Fort Lughmani; their chief said, "They are all our people, and we have brought them here to go with Mr. Rattray and fight with Meer Musjadee, near Ak Sural,

---

1. Really 400 yards.—J. C. H.
2. Query, six feet. They were in some places not more than six or seven feet; and at the officers' quarters—the highest point—probably not more than twenty feet high.— J. C. H.

about 16 miles from Lughmani." Each of them had a gun; some were loaded before they arrived, and some were loading when I saw them; about 17 chiefs were sitting in a tent with Major E. Pottinger and Mr. Rattray in a small garden beyond the fort. About 1 o'clock p. m. three of the chiefs said to Mr. Rattray, "You must take care and not come out to see people, or they will kill you; they only came here for that purpose, and to take this fort; after which they will attack the cantonments."

Mr. Rattray said, "They have all eaten our salt, and could never be guilty of such an act." Half an hour afterwards, Mr. Rattray came from the fort, and told me to come along with him to see these Kohistanees. I accompanied, with his *mirza* and a *chuprassie*.

When Mr Rattray came near them, all the chiefs paid their respects to him saying, "Inshallah, we shall go tomorrow and fight with Meer Musjadee."

Mr. R. said, "Very good, if you go, I will give you some *sowars*."

Mr. R. then turned to go back to the fort, but Jubber Khan asked him to look at his men, to which he agreed and turned back again. When he had taken about six or seven steps, one of the Kohistanees called him by name, and ran at him, firing his gun at Mr. Rattray, who turned and ran towards the fort. I, the *mirza*, and the *chuprassie* all ran towards the fort. When I had nearly reached it, I looked back. and saw Mr. Rattray lying down on the plain. I ran again towards him; and when near him he called me, and told me to take hold of him and help him into the fort.

Directly I took hold of his hand, about fifty Kohistanees fired, and Mr Rattray received a ball in his forehead; I then ran back and got into the fort, where I found Major E. Pottinger looking towards the Kohistanees and firing at them. About half-past 4 p. m. Adjutant Haugton came to the fort with two companies, and attacking the Kohistanees, killed forty or fifty, driving the rest towards the hills. Captain Codringon left about sixty *sepoys* in the fort, and returned with the remainder, to Cantonments.

The next morning (4th November) the Kohistanees collected about twelve or thirteen thousand men on the hills. Lieutenants Salusbury and Haughton came out with two companies and one gun, attacked, defeated, and dispersed the Kohistanees, but Mr. Salusbury was very badly wounded by a gunshot wound in the groin.[3] When Major E. Pottinger saw the enemy running away, he told me to take twenty *sowars* and join Lieut. Haughton, which I did. Lieut. Haughton told me to send 12 of the *sowars* to Mr. Salusbury, and to take 12 to Captain Codrington in Cantonments. When I arrived. Captain Codrington told me to remain, but to send the *sowars* after the enemy. When Lieut. Haughton and Salusbury had expended all their ammunition, they returned to cantonment, and during the night Lieutenant Salusbury died.

During the whole of this day we were fighting near cantonments, and that night the Kohistanees went back to the Fort Lughmani, which they surrounded and began to undermine. There were about twenty-four hostages, sons of different chiefs, in the fort, and we had there also 10,000 *rupees* of treasure. Major Pottinger and the doctor, with their servants and sixty *sepoys*, stole out of the fort at night and crept up to cantonments, where they arrived about 8 o'clock. When the hostages saw our party going away they remained quiet, because they thought that if they made a noise, the Kohistanees would come in and divide the treasure. When the hostages had divided the treasure, they opened the large gate, and called out to the Kohistanees to come in. On entering, all the chiefs exclaimed, "We have beaten them, and tomorrow we will take the cantonments."

On the morning of the 6th, Major Pottinger sallied out of the cantonments with a gun and two companies, and took up a position near a *nullah* from where he begun to fire at the enemy, but in half an hour he was wounded by a ball in his left foot; he then took the gun back to cantonments and left two companies.

When Captain Codrington saw that Major Pottinger was wounded, he went out to the two companies, but was very severely wounded by a shot in the back. All his *sepoys* began to cry for him; we were fighting with them until evening. About fifty or sixty *sepoys* were wounded this day, during the whole of which we had sufficient water. Captain Codrington was able to walk into cantonments, but fell down before he reached his house and asked for water; we carried him and laid him on the same bed as Major Pottinger, when he asked for pen, ink and paper, and wrote a letter to his wife whose picture he also gave to Major Pottinger. He lingered on until the night of the 7th, when he died. We buried him and Lieut. Salusbury in one grave. During the night neither our men or the enemy fired.

On the morning of the 6th, the fighting recommenced and continued until evening. That night we had water; on the morning of the 7th, Lieut. Haughton defeated the enemy, and drove them about a

---

3. Shot through the back and stomach.—J. C. H.

mile from cantonments, and we thought that they would not return any more that day. Sergeants Major Burns was shot in the groin, and died; and a great many *sepoys* and non-commissioned officers and a *jemadar* were killed: we had very little water that night, the enemy remained about one and a. half miles from us, and continued firing[4] at us, and we returned the fire all the night through.

On the morning of the 8th, Lieut. Haughton sallied out with two companies, and defeated the enemy and returned to cantonments with his men. Lieut. Haughton served out the water with his own hands this morning, quarter of a *seer* to each man. We were fighting until the evening, but at night we had not much firing from the enemy, nor did we fire.

On the 9th, the firing commenced again very sharply; this day a great many *sepoys* were killed and wounded; the *sepoys* had very little water, a quarter of *seer* to each; the enemy went to the city of Charee-kar that night.

On the morning of the 10th, we had no firing, but in the evening both parties commenced. Ensign Rose went out with two companies and killed about sixty Kohistanees, and brought in water, and one of their standards and three or four matchlocks.

On the morning of the 11th, we had very little firing, and we thought they would now go away and not attack us again. At night they fired at us to prevent our getting water. That day the *sepoys* had not a drop of water, nor until the 14th.

On the morning of the 14th, Major Pottinger,[5] Lieut. Haughton, Mr. Rose and the Doctor decided on leaving the cantonments at night, and retreating to Cabool. About 2 p. m. the *jemadar* of the *golandaze* heard of the arrangement, and determined to try and save himself by going to the enemy. He rushed on Lieut. Haughton and cut him on the hand with his sword, and then went over with his men to the enemy. About 8 p. m. we quitted cantonments and commenced our retreat to Cabool.

At about four miles we came to some water, which the *sepoys* rushed to drink, and here it was decided[6] that Major Pottinger and Lieut. Haughton, being both wounded, should ride on in front with

---

4. Long shots! Some mistake here.—J. C. H.
5. Mohun Beer was *Moonshee* to Major Pottinger, and naturally mentions him first.—J. C. H.
6. I never heard of any such proposition, and certainly would not have consented to leave my men if I had; besides they were our only protection.—J. C. H.

me, leaving the regiment to follow behind. Major Pottinger placed Mr. Rose, quarter master, and Quarter Master Sergeant Hendrigon[7] in charge of the regiment and gave orders to them to come on quickly. When we arrived near Ak Serai, we found a large *nullah* in which we concealed ourselves all day, we then mounted our horses and rode over the hills, and at 4 a. m. on the 16th we arrived at the cantonments at Cabool.

(Signed) H. M. Lawrence,
A.A.G.G.

---

7. Hanrahan. This is certainly a mistake. Pottinger led the advance, Rose and the sergeant brought up the rear, being both unwounded; the sergeant's wound had healed.—J. C. H.

Notes on Goorkhás Including the Goorkha War & Types of Ghoorkha Soldiers

Eden Vansittart

Contents

Preface   87
Geography of Népál   89
History   94
Characteristics. Religion, Arms, Dress, &c. 110
Tribes, Clans, &c.   124
Recruiting   146

THIS BOOK IS INSCRIBED BY PERMISSION
TO HIS EXCELLENCY
SIR FREDERICK SLEIGH ROBERTS, BART.,
V.C., G.C.B., G.C.I. E., R.A.,
COMMANDER-IN-CHIEF IN INDIA,
AS A SMALL TOKEN OF GRATITUDE
FOR THE GREAT INTEREST
INVARIABLY SHOWN BY HIM
IN ALL GOORKHÁ REGIMENTS.

Eden Vansittart, Capt.,
5th Goorkhás.

Simla,
2nd September 1889.

Preface

My object in writing this book has been two-fold.

1st.—I have endeavoured to gather, from all authorities on Népál and its history, such points as I hope may prove interesting.

2ndly.—I have tried to lay down, as accurately as possible, the tribes, clans, &c., of the fighting classes of Népál, together with their customs and characteristics.

In obtaining the first object, I have been much assisted by information given to me in Népál itself, and by borrowing, whenever I considered it necessary, from the following authors:—

Colonel Kirkpatrick's *Mission to Népál*, 1793.
Doctor F. Hamilton's *Account of Népál*, 1819.
Captain T. Smith's *Five Years' Residence in Népál*, from 1841 to 1845.
Captain O. Cavenagh's *Account of the Kingdom of Népál*, 1851.
Brian Hodgson's *Essays of the Language, &c., of Népál*, &c., 1874. Doctor Oldfield's *Sketches of Népál*, 1880.
Quarter Master General's No. 18 of 1883.
Confidential Report, 1884.

In my second object I have been much assisted by vernacular papers sent to me from Népál, and by the following authorities:—

Brian Hodgson's book.
Lieutenant-General R. Sale Hill's Notes, with addenda by General Sir C. Reid, K.C.B., dated 1874.
Lieutenant-Colonel E. Molloy's *Memorandum* dated Abbottabad, 1885.

I have also gathered much information from many sources whilst on recruiting duty at Gorakhpur, and have been greatly assisted especially by Subadar Jagbir Rana of the 2-4th Goorkhás, and Subadar-Major Parbal Gurung and Subadar Kulbir Thapa of the 1-5th

Goorkhás.

Eden Vansittart, Capt.,
5th Goorkhás,

United Service Club,
Simla;
2nd September 1889.

PART 1

Geography of Népál

The word "Népál" is derived from "Nai," the name of a certain god, and "*pálá*," cherished, and therefore means "cherished by Nai."
Népál is a narrow tract of country extending for about 520 miles along the southern slopes of the central portion of the Himalayas, between the 80th and 88th degree of East Longitude. Its breadth nowhere exceeds 140 miles, and averages between 90 and 100 miles.

Its general direction is from west to east, the most southern and eastern corner at the Michi River reaches as low as the 26th, whilst its most northern and western angle extends up to the 30th degree of North Latitude.

It is bounded on the north by Thibet; on the east by Sikhim and the River Michi; on the south by Bengal and the North-West Provinces; and on the west by Kumáon and the River Káli (Sárdar).

Previous to 1815 the kingdom of Népál was much more extensive, and included Kumáon and the hill country up to the River Satlej. This territory was ceded to the British by the treaty of Segowli.

The country consists of four distinct zones running east and west:

(1)—*The Terái.*—A belt of grass or *sàl* jungle, varying in breadth from 10 to 30 miles, and skirting the British frontier from the Sárdah to the Michi.

(2)—*Dhúns or Máris.*—Beyond the *sàl* forest and separating it from the second zone, *viz.*, the *Dhúns*, is the sandstone range.

This range runs in a more or less pronounced form along the whole frontier, and does not rise more than from 300 to 600 feet above its immediate base, and is from 2,000 to 3,000 feet above the level of the sea.

The "Dhúns" or "*Máris*" are valleys lying behind and below the sandstone ridge, generally at about 2,500 feet above the sea, and between the sandstone and the second range of hills.

Dehra Dhún was one of the *Dhúns*.

(3)—*Hill country.*—From the northern extremity of the "*Dhúns*," the main range of the Himalayas rises to the north; hill succeeding hill until they culminate in the snowy range. This hill region up to an elevation of 10,000 feet may be taken as the third zone.

(4)—The fourth zone is formed by the Alpine region above that altitude.

The territory of Népál, within the hills, from Kumáon in the west to Sikhim on the east, is divided into three large natural divisions, by four very lofty and massive ridges, which respectively are given off from the high peaks of Nunda Devi (25,700'), Dewalgiri (26,826'), Gosainthan (26,305'), and Kinchinjanga (28,156').

(Mount Everest lies about midway between the two last, and is 29,000 feet, but throws off no main ridges.)

These four enormous ridges stand out at right angles from the central axis of the Himalayas, and run parallel to each other nearly due south towards the plains. Each of these three natural divisions into which Népál is divided by these lofty ridges is walled in on all four sides by mountain barriers—on the north by the snowy range, on the south by the chain of sandstone hills, and on the east and west by one of the above ridges.

Each of these districts thus walled in forms a large mountain basin, sloping gradually to the south, and furrowed by numerous mountain streams which rise in the surrounding amphitheatre of mountains. All these flow towards the plains, and all converge towards each other in their course through the hills, so decidedly, that they unite into one large river in two out of three districts, before they reach even the sandstone range of hills.

Each of these three mountain basins derives its name from the river by which it is drained. Thus:—

1st.—Western division, or mountain basin of the Karnali or Gogra.

2nd.—Central division, or mountain basin of the Gandak.

3rd.—Eastern division, or mountain basin of the Kosi.

Besides these three grand geographical divisions, there are a fourth and fifth, *viz.*—

4th.—The Népál Valley.

5th.—The Terái.

The Népál Valley is formed by the bifurcation of the ridge running south from Gosainthan, thus forming an isolated triangle; it is watered by the Bhágmati, which drains the whole of this district.

The valleys formed by the numerous streams running down from the snowy watershed, are, in the lower portion, thickly inhabited and well cultivated. The most populous valleys are at an elevation of about 4,000 feet, but cultivation is carried on in the interior up to 13,000 feet.

The principal rivers of Népál from west to east come as follows:—
The Káli (or Sárdah), the Karnáli, the Rapti, the Gandak, the Bhágmati, the Kosi, and the Michi.

As already explained, Népál is divided into five divisions, *viz.*—
1. The Western.
2. The Central.
3. The Eastern.
4. The Népál Valley.
5. The Terái.

The Western division is inhabited by Doti and other non- Goorkhá tribes.

The Eastern by Limbus and Rais.

The Terái by a race called Tárús, a puny, ill-made race, and chiefly employed as *mahouts, dâk*-runners, &c.

The Central division has been called from time immemorial, by the Népálese, the Sápt Gandaki, or "country of the seven Gandaks," and lies among the seven main streams which uniting form the Gandak River; by these the whole hill country between Dewalgiri and Gosainthan is drained.

These seven rivers, known collectively as Sápi Gandaki, are, taking them successively from west to east,—

(1) The Barijai; (2) the Narayani; (3) the Sweti Gandaki; (4) the Marsiangdi; (5) the Daramdi; (6) the Gandi; and (7) the Trisul ganga.

The central division is the home of the Magars and Gurungs, and it is practically from this portion of Népál that all recruits for the British service are enlisted.

Towards the close of the last century the central division included in its limits, besides the kingdom of Goorkhá proper, 24 other independent principalities, collectively called the Chawbisi Ráj, or country of the 24 kings. These principalities were called—

Lámzúng	Rising	Botwál	Músikot
Tanhúng	Ghiring	Gúlmi	Argha
Galkot	Dhoar	Nayakot	Pyúng
Malibam	Pálpá	Kháchi	Latahúng
Sathúng	Pokra	Isma	Kaikho
Garhúng	Bhirkot	Dharkot	Piuthan.

These petty states were all overrun by the Goorkhás, shortly after their conquest of the Népál Valley, and by them divided into five provinces, called (1) Malibam, (2) Kháchi, (3) Pálpá, (4) Goorkhá, (5) Pokra.

The valley of Népál, or Népál proper, is completely surrounded by mountains which vary in altitude from 5,000 to 8,000 feet above the level of the sea.

It is of an oval shape, with an average length of 15 miles, with an average breadth of 13 miles. The area is about 250 square miles. The British Residency is 4,700 feet above the sea. The Népál Valley is densely populated and is supposed to contain nearly 300,000 souls, most of whom are Newárs and Murmis.

It is well supplied with water by numberless streams, which all converge towards the central long axis and join the Bhágmatti River.

Katmandu, the capital of Népál, is an immense city, and here live in different palaces the king, the prime minister, and all great officials.

It is impossible to calculate with any accuracy the area of Népál, but it is supposed to be about 54,000 square miles.

The population of Népál is estimated by the Népálese at from 5,200,000 to 5,600,000, and by most writers at about 4,000,000. It is impossible to form any correct estimate of the population, but the best authority calculates it at not more than 2,000,000.

The revenue of Népál is supposed to be about ten *lakhs* of rupees, but the writer thinks it must be nearer 20 *lakhs*. The grains produced in the lowlands of Népál are Indian-corn, rice, wheat, barley, millet, pulses of various kinds, and an enormous amount of red pepper.

Of fruits the chief are the pineapple, orange, guava, plantain, and pomegranate. Of vegetables the principal are garlic, cabbages, peas, turnips, ginger, and sugarcane.

In the mountain regions the peach, apricot, walnut, raspberry, and wild strawberry are found. These parts also are rich in mines of iron, lead, and copper, and it is said that gold mines also exist.

There are some coal-mines not far from Botwál, and also close to Tribeni, as the writer of this obtained some specimen bits, through some recruiters, in 1889. He submitted the same for examination to the Chief Agent of the Bengal and North-western Railway, who pronounced them to be very good coal.

An enormous amount of *sál* wood is annually cut in the Terái, and this forms one of the principal sources of income to the Népál Government.

The Thibetans bring down for sale in Népál blankets of various kinds, and other woollen manufactures; also ponies, watch-dogs,— large hairy beasts, about the size of an ordinary Newfoundland dog— goats, sheep, agate, turquoise, yák-tails, gold-dust, gold and silver ore, and quantities of rock-salt.

The salt is packed in bags forming loads of about 15lb. each, which are brought across the snows fastened to the backs of sheep.

All mines in Népál are worked by the Agrái tribe, who must find it a paying business, as a proverb exists in Népál which says, Karipút o Rániput (a miner's son and a prince's son).

PART 2

History

The aboriginal stock of Népál is most undoubtedly Turanian. This fact is inscribed in very plain characters in their faces, forms, and languages.

Amongst the aborigines of Népál must be counted the Newárs, Magars, Gurungs, Kiránts or Rais, Limbus, and Lepchas: these are all Turanians.

The Magars have for many centuries more or less admitted the supremacy of the doctrines of the Bráhmans, and consequently they have adopted many Rájpút customs, ceremonies, and names. The Gurungs also, but to a very much lesser degree, have borrowed from the Rájpúts, but this does not give either of these two tribes any claim to any other descent than Turanian.

The Newárs inhabited the "Valley of Népál" or "Népál Proper." Their early history, like that of most Eastern nations, is buried in a mass of fables. The inhabitants exhibit a list of princes for several thousand years back, which is given in Colonel Kirkpatrick's work, but without much evidence of its authenticity.

The Gurungs inhabited the country about Lámzúng, Ghándrung, and Siklis. The Magars were south of the Gurungs, and about Gúlmi, Arghá, Káchi, and Pálpá, and the Rais and Limbus inhabited the whole of the country to the north and to the east of the Népál Valley. The Lepchas are the inhabitants of Sikhim.

About the ancient history of these tribes nothing is known.

We know, however, that Népál never was subjected by the Delhi emperors or by any other of the great Asiatic conquerors.

It is stated by Colonel Todd that the Goorkhá dynasty was founded towards the end of the 12th century by the third son of the Rájpút Rájáh Samarsi, Ruler of Chitor,[1] who settled in Pálpá.

1. This would account for the numerous Chitoriah clans.

A Népálese tradition exists which says that the Rájáh of Udeipur, probably Hari Sing, was besieged by the Mahomedans in his capital. He made a long and gallant defence, but at last food and water began to fail him, and foreseeing the horrors of famine, he destroyed all the women and children within the city, to the number of 70,000, set fire to the town, and with his garrison attacked and cut his way through the Mahomedan hosts, and took refuge in the hills of Népál to the west of the Gandak River, where he was hospitably received by the aborigines.

Whatever truth there may be in the above traditions, there can be no doubt that the large numbers of Rájpúts and Bráhmans did make their appearance in Western Népál about the twelfth century, and it can easily be understood how in time, from their superior intelligence and civilization, they obtained positions of influence and importance amongst the barbarians who inhabited the land.

In time it would appear that a number of the Magar mountaineer princes were persuaded to follow the doctrines of the Bráhmans, and many of the subjects and clans of these princes were induced to follow the example set them, but a large number also refused to be converted.

To the former the Bráhmans granted the sacred thread, whilst they denied it to the latter, and hence have sprung up tribes called Thápás, Ghartis, Ránás, &c., &c., some of whom wear the thread and are called Khas, whilst the others do not wear the thread and remain merely Magars.

The Bráhmans, to completely reconcile their most important converts, worked out marvellous pedigrees for them, and gave them the right to claim descent from various famous origins, such as "*Súrja Bansi*," "born of the sun," "born of the moon," "born of a king," &c., &c.

The progeny of the women of the country by Bráhmans were as a term of reproach called "*Khas*," or the "fallen," from "*Khasna*," "to fall," but the Bráhmans invested this progeny with the sacred thread also, and thereby gave them a higher social standing than the Magars and Gurungs. But this is most clearly and graphically described by Brian Hodgson.

After describing how the Mahomedan conquest and bigotry continued to drive multitudes of Bráhmans from the plains of Hindustan to the proximate hills, which now form the western territories of Népál, Brian Hodgson says—

The Bráhmans found the natives illiterate, and without faith, but fierce and proud. They saw that the barbarians had vacant minds, ready to receive their doctrines, but spirits not apt to stoop to degradation, and they acted accordingly. To the earliest and most distinguished of their converts they communicated, in defiance of the creed, they taught, the lofty rank and honours of the Kshatriya order.

But the Bráhmans had sensual passions to gratify, as well as ambition. They found the native females—even of the most distinguished—nothing loth, but still of a temper, like that of the males, prompt to resent indignities.

These females would indeed welcome the polished Bráhmans to their embraces, but their offspring must not be stigmatized as the infamous progeny of a Bráhman and a Mléchha. To this progeny also, then the Brahmans, in still greater defiance of their creed communicated the rank of the second order of Hinduism; and from these two roots (converts and illegitimate progeny), mainly, spring the now numerous, predominant, and extensively ramified, tribe of *Khas*, originally the name of a small clan of creedless barbarians, now the proud title of Kshatriya, or military order of the Kingdom of Népál. The offspring of the original *Khas* females and of Bráhmans, with the honours and rank of the second order of Hinduism, got the patronymic titles of the first order; and hence the key to the anomalous nomenclature of so many stirpes of the military tribes of Népál is to be sought in the nomenclature of the sacred order.

It may be added, as remarkably illustrative of the lofty spirit of the *parbattias* (Highlanders), that, in spite of the yearly increasing sway of Hinduism in Népál, and the various attempts of the Bráhmans in high office to procure the abolition of a custom so radically opposed to the creed both parties now profess, the Khas still insist that the fruit of commerce (marriage is out of the question) between their females and males of the sacred order shall be ranked as Kshatriya, wear the thread, and assume the patronymic title.

The famous Prime Minister Bhim Sen was the descendant of a Magar Thápá, as was also General Amar Sing.

Now, as has been shown, from the advent of these thousands of foreigners and their numerous progeny sprang up a new race, called Khas, and with this new race also came a new language, a kind of Hindi *patois*, which was called the language of the Khas, or Khas-

Khúra, which is nowadays the *"lingua franca"* of Népál.

Doctor F. Hamilton, in his book published in 1819, says that the Magars who resided in the hills to the west of the Gandak River seem to have received the Rájpút princes with much cordiality.

They have submitted to the guidance of the Bráhmans, but formerly had priests of their own, and seemed to have worshipped chiefly ghosts.

Near the Magars was settled a numerous tribe named Gurungs, whose manners are in most respects nearly the same with those of the Magars. This tribe was very much addicted to arms.

It would appear that a Gurung chief, who was Rájáh of Káski, settled in Ghándrúng, where the Gurungs were most predominant. These people were strongly attached to his descendants, by whom they were not disturbed in their religious opinions or customs, and in their own homes they practically still continue to follow the doctrines of Sakia as explained to them by *Lámás* of their own tribe.

No Gurungs have as yet ever been admitted to the dignity of Khas, but with their constant intercourse with the Khas, who are Hindus, their original faith is getting weaker and in time will disappear.

It may here be pointed out that none of the high-sounding titles which are to be found amongst the Magars, and which were evidently brought in by the Bráhmans from Hindustan, are to be found amongst the Gurungs.

Amongst the thousands of Goorkhás the writer has seen, he has never met a Surja Bansi Gurung, and he doubts the existence of any.

The district of Goorkhá is situated in the north-east portion of the basin of the Gandak, occupying the country between the Trisulganga and the Sweti Gandak.

The chief town is called Goorkhá, and is about 55 miles to the west of Katmandu.

This town, and eventually the district, is said to have obtained its name from a very famous saint called Gorkhánát, or Gorákhánát, who resided in a cave, which still exists, in the hill in which the city of Gorkhá is built.

The ancestors of the present race of Goorkhás derived their national name of Goorkhá from this district, in which they first established themselves as an independent power. The term Goorkhá is not limited to any particular class or clan; it is applied to all those whose ancestors inhabited the country of Goorkhá, and who from it, subsequently, extended their conquests far and wide over the eastern and western hills.

The men of Doti, Jumla, and other western portions of Nepál and the Kumáon hills, are *parbattias* (Highlanders), but they are not Goorkhás, and never were so, whilst Damáis and Sárkhis are recognized as "Gorkhális," notwithstanding their very low social standing, from the mere fact of their ancestors having resided in the Goorkhá district.

In 1802 Docter F. Hamilton writes:

The first persons of the Goorkhá family of whom I have heard were two brothers, named Khancha[2] and Mincha, words altogether barbarous, denoting their descent from a Magar family, and not from the Pamars, as they pretend.

Khancha was the founder of the imperial branch of the family, *viz.*, they remained Magars. Mincha was the chief of Nayakot and adopted the Hindu rules of purity, and his descendants intermarried with the best families, although not without creating disgust.

The Khancha family possessed Bhirkot, Gharhung, and Dhor.

Bhirkot seems to have been the head of the whole, as its chief was at the head of a league containing Nayakot.

Mincha, the Rájáh of Nayakot, and the chiefs of this place, although they lived pure, continued to the last to follow in war the impure representatives of Khancha.

A branch of the Mincha family ruled at Káski. The Chief of Lámzúng was descended from a younger son of the Káski ruler, and in time became very powerful, and he was followed in war not only by his kinsman, the Chief of Káski, but by the Rájáh of Tanahung.

One of the Lámzúng rájáhs had a younger brother, Darbha Sáhi, who rebelled and took to himself Goorkhá, which then formed the southern part of the principality. The capital Goorkhá is situated on a very high hill and contains the temple of Gorákhánát. From this we may infer that the proper name of the place is Goorakhá, and that previous to having adopted the doctrines of the Bráhmans, this family had received the *"jogis,"* or priest, of Gorákhánát as their spiritual guides.

The first chief of Goorkhá, was Darbha Sáhi, and his descendants were as follows:

1, Rámá Sáhi; 2, Puran Sáhi; 3, Chatra Sáhi; 4, Dambar Sáhi; 5, Birbhadra Sáhi; 6, Prithwi Pati Sáhi; 7, Nribhupal Sáhi. These chiefs

---

2. *"Khancha"* is the Khus Khúra for "younger brother".

entered into none of the leagues formed by their neighbour, but trusted entirely to their own vigour.

Nribhupal Sáhi procured in marriage, first, a daughter of the Pálpá family, and secondly, a daughter of the chief of Malibam.

His eldest son, Prithwi Narain Sáhi, was a person of insatiable ambition, sound judgement, great courage, and unceasing activity. He is practically the great founder of the house of Goorkhá. It would appear that in the earlier days of Prithwi Narain's reign, the inhabitants of the district of Goorkhá were almost entirely Magars, Gurungs, Thakhúrs, and Khas, with a sprinkling of the menial classes.

In the year 1749 one of the princes in Népál proper, who was King of Bhatgáon, was ill-advised enough to apply for assistance to Prithwi Narain against his enemies, rival princes, who were pressing him hard.

Prithwi Narain had been extending his own dominions on all sides, and was only too glad to have an opportunity of establishing a secure footing in Népál, and he therefore advanced at once from Goorkhá with an army of Magars, Gurungs, Khas, and Thákúrs.

Ranjit Mal soon found out his mistake, and was obliged to come to terms with the neighbouring kings, with a view to resist the encroachments of the Goorkhás.

Prithwi Narain, however, had occupied the hills round the valley, and established a series of small forts on them, the ruins of which exist to this day.

Finding himself not strong enough to seize the valley, he blockaded it, and at length, in 1769 A.D., descended into the level country and attacked Kirtapúr, a town belonging to the Petan Rájáh. Aided by the King of Katmandu, the inhabitants defeated the Goorkhás, killing a brother of Prithwi Narain.

Shortly afterwards the Goorkhá King made another attack in Kirtapúr, but was again defeated.

After subduing some neighbouring petty states, he again besieged Kirtapúr, and obtained entrance to the town by treachery.

After taking Kirtapúr he proceeded to attack Petan, but was obliged to raise the siege in order to oppose Major Kinloch, to whom the Népálese applied for assistance.

Major Kinloch's force being inadequate for the purpose, and being still further weakened by sickness, was repulsed by the Goorkhás, who then returned and attacked Katmandu.

Prithvi Narain obtained possession of Katmandu by treachery, and then successively of Bhatgaon and Petan, thus completing the conquest of Népál in 1769 A.D.

Prithwi Narain died in 1771 and left two sons, Sing Pertab and Bahádar Sah, the former of whom succeeded his father.

Sing Pertab died in 1775, leaving one legitimate son, Ran Bahddar Sah, who at the time of his father's death was but an infant. On the death of Sing Pertab, his broher Bahádar Sah became regent.

The mother of the infant king opposed him, and after a struggle of some years Bahádar Sah had to fly to Bettiáh, where he remained until 1795, when the *Rani* died and he again became Regent.

In 1790 the Goorkhás invaded Thibet and pillaged Lhása.

In 1792 a Chinese army of 70,000 men invaded Népál by the Kirong route, and after some desperate fights, overcame the Népálese, and dictated terms to the Goorkhá King at Nayakot, some 25 miles from Katmandu.

In March 1792 Lord Cornwallis entered into a commercial treaty with the Goorkhás.

In consequence of this, a mission under Colonel Kirkpatrick was despatched to Népál the same year. In 1793 Colonel Kirkpatrick quitted Népál, as he found the Népálese determined to avoid a closer alliance.

In 1793 the Goorkhás under Jagajit conquered Kumáon.[3]

In 1794 the Goorkhás under Amar Sing conquered and annexed Gharwál. They next fought the Gharwális in the Dún near Gúrúdhana, utterly defeated them, killed their *rájáh*, and annexed the Dún, which had belonged to the Gharwális.

By this time the Goorkhá territories extended from Bhútán to Kashmir, and from the borders of Thibet to the British provinces.

In 1795 Ran Bahádar Sah removed his uncle from the regency and assumed the reins of government: two years subsequently he put him to death.

From this time till 1800 Népál was the scene of most barbarous outrages perpetrated by the King.

In 1800 Ran Bahádar Sah was expelled from the country and obliged to abdicate in favour of his illegitimate son, who was still an infant.

In October 1801 a treaty was signed by the British and Népálese authorities, and in consequence of Népál. Captain W. D. Knox was

---

3. Kurmáon and Gharwál remained subject to the Goorkhás until 1816, when they were ceded to the British by the treaty of Segowli.

appointed Resident at the Court of Népál, and he reached the capital in April 1802.

Becoming dissatisfied with the political conduct of the Népálese, who evaded the fulfilment of their engagements, he withdrew in March 1803. In January 1804 Lord Wellesley formally dissolved alliance with the Durbar.

From this time until 1814, the Népálese carried on a system of outrage and encroachment on the British frontier.

On the 1st November 1814, Lord Hastings declared war against Népál, on account of these continual outrages and encroachments, which culminated in the treacherous attack and murder of all our police in the Botwál district.

The Goorkhá army consisted of 12,000 men, equipped and disciplined in imitation of the Company's *sepoys*.

When war was determined on, 30,000 British troops with 60 guns were told off in four divisions.

The war, though ultimately brought to a successful termination by the brilliant operations of Ochterlony, was one very discreditable to the military abilities of our generals; yet it reflected the highest credit to the troops employed, being perhaps the most arduous campaign in which the Company's army had ever been engaged in India.

Throughout the war the Goorkhás displayed the most conspicuous gallantry.

Major-General Gillespie, advancing from Meerut, seized the Keeri Pass over the Sewaliks and occupied Dehra without opposition. Five miles from Dehra is a hill 500 to 600 feet high, surmounted with a fort called Nálápáni or Kalunga, of no great size or strength.

The defence of this post against General Gillespie was most creditable to the Goorkhás, though exhibiting extreme rashness on his part, as he had been directed to avoid strong works which required to be reduced by artillery.

In this defence Balbhadar and [4]600 Goorkhás repulsed two assaults, inflicting on the British division a loss of 31 officers and 750 men killed and wounded, including General Gillespie, who was killed when leading the first assault; and when ultimately three days' incessant shelling compelled them to abandon the place, Balbhadar and the survivors, reduced to go in number, cut their way through our posts, and escaped.

---

4. These 600 men belonged mostly to the regiment known as the Purána Gorakh, which consists entirely of Magars.

The defence of this fort retarded a whole division for over one month.

On the fall of the fort it was at once occupied by the British troops, and there indeed the desperate courage and bloody resistance the Goorkhás had opposed to means so overwhelming were mournfully and horribly apparent. The whole area of the fort was a slaughter-house strewed with the bodies of the dead and wounded.

The determined resolution of the little party that held this small post must surely claim universal admiration.

The men of Nálápáni (or Kalinga) will forever be marked for their unsubdued courage, and the generous spirit of courtesy with which they treated their enemy.

They fought us in fair conflict like men, and in the intervals of actual combat showed us a liberal courtesy worthy of a more enlightened people; so far from insulting the bodies of the dead and wounded, they permitted them to remain untouched till carried away, and none were stripped even. The following story illustrates their confidence in British officers. One day whilst the batteries were playing, a man was perceived on the breach advancing and waving his hand. The guns ceased for a while, and a man came, who proved to be a Goorkhá, whose lower jaw had been shattered by a round shot and who came thus frankly to solicit assistance from his enemy.

It is unnecessary to add that it was instantly afforded. He recovered, and when discharged from the hospital, signified his desire to return to his corps to fight us again, exhibiting thus through the whole a strong sense of the value of generosity and courtesy in warfare, and also of his duty to his country, separating completely in his own mind private and national feeling from each other.

During the assaults on the fort, women were seen hurling stones, and undauntedly exposing themselves; and several of their dead bodies, and one wounded, were subsequently found amidst the ruins of the fort.

Balbhadar with the survivors retreated to a hill a few miles distant, and was there joined by 300 fresh Goorkhás, and subsequently he formed a part of the garrison of Jythak.

On General Gillespie's death, General Martindell was given the command of the division.

He left a detachment in the Dún, and entered the valley below Náhan by the Kolápari pass on 19th December 1814.

Náhan was found evacuated and was thereupon occupied by the

British. Colonel Kesar Sing, who had been in Náhan with 2,300 of the *élite* of the Goorkhá army, had retired to Jythak, in accordance with General Amar Sing's orders.

General Martindell sent two detachments, one of 738 men under Major Richards, and the other of 1,000 men under Major Ludlow, to occupy two ridges on the flanks of the enemy's main position.

The detachment under Major Ludlow attacked the enemy and drove them off with some loss; but being flushed with success he pursued too far, and on seeing a stockade in front of him, he attempted to seize the same and failed. This stockade was afterwards always known as the second stockade.

The officer commanding the stockade seeing the disordered state of our troops, and how few of them there were together, sallied out with no great number of men, bore down the leading troops, and put the rest to flight. Reinforced by fresh troops, the enemy followed up the charge, and our men, out of breath and panic-struck, could not be rallied. Major Ludlow and other officers three times attempted to rally the troops at favourable points, but as often the Goorkhás charged and dispersed them, and followed, cutting them up with their *kúkries*.

In the meanwhile the other detachment under Major Richards made good its object, but owing to the failure of Major Ludlow's column, they were ordered to retreat.

Lieutenant Thakery, with a company of the 26th Native Infantry, made a gallant charge to cover the retreat; but the enemy breaking their way in on all sides, and using their *kúkries*, committed terrible havoc. The British loss was 12 officers and 450 men killed and wounded. In February 1815 Ranjin Sing with 200 Goorkhás attacked and defeated 2,000 irregulars under Lieutenant Young,

The fall of Jythak was only brought about by the successes of General Ochterlony and the surrender of Amar Sing,

General T. Wood, who commanded a division at Gorakhpur, having heard that the enemy under Colonel Wajir Sing held a stockade called Jitghar, close to Botwál, determined to attack the same.

He advanced for this purpose on the 3rd of January 1815. The route led for the last seven miles through *sál* forests. General Wood had been told to expect an open space in front of the stockade, but whilst still in the thick of the forest, he suddenly found himself in front of the stockade, and within 50 yards of it. A destructive fire was opened on the British troops. The stockade was merely a hollow one, and a position was gained round the left flank completely commanding the stockade: the carrying of the work was certain and the enemy were already retreating from it, when General Wood ordered the retreat to be sounded! The British lost 5 officers and 128 men killed and wounded. General Wood did nothing from this date until 17th of April, when he made a useless demonstration against Botwál, with no results.

General Marley was expected to attempt the Bichiakoh and Hetounda pass, and, if successful, from thence straight on to Katmandu. He occupied several posts in the *Terái* and kept his main army at Parsa. One post, held by Captain Sibley, was 20 miles to the left of Parsa, and another under Captain Blackney at Summarpúr, about as far to the right.

The main army of the Goorkhás was at Makwanpúr under Colonel Randhar Sing, who gave orders that both these posts should be attacked on the 1st January 1815.

Captain Blackney was completely surprised, and he and Lieutenant Duncan were killed, and in ten minutes his *sepoys* broke and fled in every direction. Captain Sibley was more on his guard, and made a good fight of it, but was surrounded and overpowered.

Our loss out of 500 men, was 123 killed, 187 wounded, and 73 missing.

General Marley was superseded for incompetence, and Lieutenant Pickersgill General George Wood took command in his stead. The very day before assuming command. Lieutenant Pickersgill, with a body of cavalry, surprised a body of 500 Goorkhás and cut nearly all up.

General George Wood had a fine army of 13,400 men, but being of opinion that the fever season had commenced, he refused to risk penetrating the forest, and accordingly he did nothing.

In December 1814 Lord Hastings, considering that a diversion from Kumáon might have a good effect, gave orders to Colonel Gardner and Major Hearsey to raise two levies composed of Rohillas.

Colonel Gardner advanced on the 11th February from Kashipur in the Moradabad district, and after some skirmishing established himself on 20th February 1815 on a ridge immediately facing Almorah.

About the same time Major Hearsey advanced through Pilibhit and moved on towards Almorah, with the intention of co-operating with Colonel Gardner, but on 31st March he was defeated in an engagement and he himself was wounded and taken prisoner.

Towards the end of March, Colonel Jasper Nichols was sent with 2,500 infantry and 10 guns to support Colonel Gardner. After the junction was effected a good deal of fighting took place round Almorah. By 25th April guns had been put up in a position within 70 yards of the fort. The Governor of the province thereupon proposed an armistice. On the 27th a formal convention was signed, in which the whole Kumáon province was surrendered, and Major Hearsey was released.

General Ochterlony, who took the field in the middle of October, had 7,000 troops under him, and was opposed by General Amar Sing, who never had more than from 2,800 to 3,000 Goorkhás under him.

General Ochterlony determined to act with the utmost caution, and by his perseverance and skilful operations, he was enabled to outmanoeuvre Amar Sing from position to position. Up till the middle of February nothing of much importance was done. Between this and the 14th April, a number of small forts were reduced. On the 15th April, after some very hard fighting, the British troops seized a peak called Deothal, in the very heart of the enemy's position, and therein placed two whole battalions with two field pieces, and threw up earthworks all round the same.

Amar Sing seeing the absolute necessity of dislodging the British from Deothal, attacked the same on the 16th with 2,000 Goorkhás, led by Bhagti Thápá.

The attack took place from all sides with furious intrepidity, but the enemy were repulsed with a loss of 500 men, Bhagti Thápá being killed. The British lost 7 officers and 347 men killed and wounded.

The Goorkhás now concentrated round Maláon, but news of the fall of Almorah having arrived, Amar Sing's *sirdars* urged him to accept terms for himself and his son Ranjit at Jythak, This he refused to do, and as the chiefs began to desert him, he retired into Maláon with 200 men, and there held out as long as any hope remained, after which he capitulated on highly honourable terms to General Ochterlony.

The gallant defence of Fort Maláon by Amar Sing elicited the admiration of General Ochterlony, who allowed him to march out with his arms, accoutrements, colours, two guns, and all his personal property, "in consideration of the bravery, skill, and fidelity with which he had defended the country entrusted to his charge": the same honourable terms were granted to his son, who had defended Jythak against General Martindell,

The fort of Maláon brought the campaign of 1814-15 to an end.

Negotiations for peace were now opened in May 1815, but the refusal of the Népálese to submit to Lord Hastings' demands led to the campaign of 1816.

General Ochterlony advanced with 20,000 troops early in February against the Bichakoh pass, which he found impregnable. Fortunately he was able to turn this position, on 14th February 1816, by means of a very rugged road, which was unknown to the enemy, and was shown to him by some smugglers.

On the 27th an advance was made upon and a position taken up in front of Makwánpur. On the 28th 2,000 Goorkhás attacked a post called Sekha Khatri, situated on a hill to the left of the camp. The village was obstinately and gallantly defended by the small detachment there; General Ochterlony successively detached one European and three Native battalions in support, and after a most obstinate fight the enemy was beaten off. The British casualties were two officers and 222 men, but the loss of the enemy was over 800.

On the 1st March a strong point 800 yards from the Goorkhá stockade on the hill on which Harihárpúr stands was surprised and the Goorkhá picquet driven off.

The Goorkhás, in considerable numbers, made a most desperate and obstinate attempt to recover this position. It was impossible, owing to the nature of the ground, to use the bayonet, and the musketry fire lasted from 3 a.m. till 11.30, when the arrival of some guns at last drove the enemy away, after several hours of hard fighting. British loss five officers and 54 men.

After the war of 1816, Sir D. Ochterlony expressed an opinion confidentially to Lord Hastings that "the Company's soldiers, then Hindustanis, could never be brought to resist the shock of these energetic mountaineers on their own ground."

The intelligence of their reverses at Sekha Khatri and Harihárpúr spread consternation at Katmandu, and the Durbar immediately tendered, unqualified submission; and thus was ended the second war in a short and brilliant campaign.

On the 4th March the treaty of Segowli was signed, by which Népál was reduced to the country lying between the River Michi on the east and the River Kali on the west, and by this treaty they also ceded nearly the whole *Terái* west of the Gandak River to the British.

In fulfilment of the terms of this treaty, a British Resident was appointed, Mr. Gardner being selected. The King was at this time still young, and Bhim Sen Thápá held the reins of government.

The King died in his 18th year, shortly after Mr. Gardner's arrival, and his successor was only 2 years old.

Bhim Sen Thápá retained complete and uninterrupted power until 1832.

In 1833 the King, instigated by the queen, endeavoured, but without success, to free himself from the rule of Bhim Sen Thápá. The attempt was renewed in 1836, and in 1837 Bhim Sen Thápá was removed from office and imprisoned. He was, however, soon released, but never regained his former position, and in 1839 he was again put in irons. Threats were made that his wife and female relatives would be shamefully treated in public, and preferring to die rather than witness the disgrace, Bhim Sen Thápá committed suicide in prison. So ended the life of a gallant old chief, who had ruled the country for 26 years.

In 1843 Matbar Sing Thápá, the nephew of Bhim Sen Thápá, who was in exile in the Punjab, was recalled and made prime minister.

In 1845 he was murdered at the instigation of one Gagan Sing, a great favourite of the *Maháráni*.

The murder of Gagan Sing and thirty-one of the most influential chiefs, in 1846, paved the way for Jang Bahádar.

Finding that Jang Bahádar was not so subservient to her purposes as she expected, the *Maháráni* endeavoured to compass his death, but failing, she was expelled with her two sons from the country, and was accompanied to Benares by the *Mahárájáh*, who returned to Népál the following year, only to abdicate in favour of the heir-apparent, Surendar Bikram.

In 1848 an offer was made to the British Government to assist in the war with the Sikhs, but the offer was declined.

On the 15th of January 1850 Jang Bahádar started to visit England.

In 1854 the Népálese entered into war with Thibet, which lasted two years, and terminated favourably for Népál. Dr. Oldfield gives the following details:—

The first week in April about 1,000 Goorkhás under General Dher Sham Sher (the father of the present Prime Minister Mahárájáh Bir Sham Sher Rana Bahadur, [at time of first publication]) attacked a body of about from 3,000 to 5,000 Thibetans and defeated them.

On the 26th news arrived of a victory gained by the Goorkhás. It would appear that a large body of Thibetans occupied a post called Ganta, about eight miles from Jhanga. For nine days the Thibetans repulsed with considerable loss the successive attacks of the Goorkhás, but at length they were driven out of the post, which was occupied at once by the Goorkhás.

On the 4th May news arrived that the Goorkhás had captured the post of Jhanga.

In November news arrived that a very large force of Thibetans and Tartars had surprised the Goorkhá position at Kuti, to which place they had retired at the commencement of the rains. The Goorkhás were, after several hours' hard fighting, utterly routed and lost 700 men killed and nine guns.

Only 1,300 Goorkhás escaped.

On the 19th November the Thibetans attacked Jhanga at night and entered the position, but after some hours' fighting they were driven out and defeated, leaving 1,200 dead behind them.

On the 25th November news arrived that General Dher Sham Sher with five to six thousand Goorkhás, divided into nine regiments, advanced against Kuti. The Thibetans were in an entrenched camp, and numbered about 10,000. After some good hard fighting they were defeated with a loss of 1,100 killed. The Goorkhás here recovered two of the guns they had lost.

Colonel Sanak Sing with five regiments attacked the Thibetans near Jhanga and killed over 1,100 chiefly with the *kukry*.

The force in Jhanga killed 559 Thibetans; after these reverses the Thibetans submitted.

In 1857, when the mutiny broke out, the Népálese offered the assistance of their troops to the British Government, and the same was accepted on the 26th June.

On the 2nd July, 3,000 troops were sent off to the plains of India, and 1,000 more followed on the 13th and 14th August. On the 10th December, Jang Bahádar himself went down with a force of 8,000. This force was joined by Colonel Macgregor as Military Commissioner, and assisted in the campaign of 1857 and 1858. Early in 1858 numbers of fugitive rebels took refuge in the Népálese Terái. In 1859 the Népálese organized an expedition, and swept the remnant of the mutineers out of the country.

In return for the above services, Jang Bahádar was created a G.C.B., and under a treaty concluded on 1st November 1860 the tract of country on the Oudh frontier, which had been ceded to the British Government in 1816, was restored to Népál.

In 1878 Sir Jang Bahádar died from the effects of injuries received from a tiger he had wounded whilst out shooting.

Ranodhip Sing, a brother of Jang Bahádar's, then became Prime Minister until 22nd November 1885, when he was assassinated and his nephew Bir Sham Sher Rana Bahádar, the present Prime Minister, (at time of first publication), took up the reins of Government.

The Népálese army is said to consist of 30,000 drilled soldiers including artillery, who are almost all paid in land. They are drilled according to the English drill book and with English words of command.

At a parade held in Katmandu on 6th March 1888, 108 guns marched past the Prime Minister, and it is therefore only natural to conclude that the Népálese, considering their small army, are strong in this branch.

Several regiments are now (1889) armed with Henry Martinis manufactured in the country. More are being daily manufactured, and it would appear the whole army is to receive them. There are also a number of Népálese-made Sniders, and some thousands of Enfields, either captured from the mutineers in 1859, or given by the British Government.

PART 3

Characteristics. Religion, Arms, Dress, &c.

About 600 years before Christ it is said that Sakya Singha (Buddha—the wise one) visited the Népál Valley, and found that the fundamental principles of his religion had already been introduced amongst the Newars by Manjasri from China.

To Manjasri by the Buddhists, and to Vishnu by the Hindus, are assigned, respectively, the honour of having by a miracle converted the large mountain lake of Nága Vása into the present fertile Népál Valley, by cutting with one blow of a sword the pass by which the Bhágmati River leaves the valley of Népál. To this day (at time of first publication), this pass is called "Kot bar," "Sword cut."

It is known as a fact that 300 years before Christ, Buddhism flourished in Népál, and it is still nominally the faith of the majority of Newars (some Newars have been Hindus from time immemorial); yet it is steadily being supplanted by Hinduism, and before another century it will have entirely disappeared.

The Khas are Hindus. The Magars and Gurungs are so also nominally, but their Hinduism is not very strict.

The Gurungs in their own country are really Buddhists, though they would not admit it in India.

To this day their priests in their own homes are *Lámás* and *Giábrings*, but when serving in our regiments they submit to the Bráhmans and employ them for all priestly functions.

The fashionable religion is Hinduism, and it may therefore be said that Goorkhás are Hindus, and with them, therefore, Bráhmans are the highest caste, from whose hands no impurity can come. The Bráhmans wear the thread (*Tania*).

In the case of Bráhman with Khas, or Khas with lower grades, there can be no marriage.

Neither can a Magar marry a Gurung or *vice versâ*, nor can a Solábját Gurung marry into the Chárját or *vice versâ*.

The offspring of an Opadia Bráhman with a Bráhman's widow is called "*Jaici*."

That of a *Jaici*, and certain Bráhmans with a Khas, is called *Khattri*. The *Khattri* wears the thread, but is below the Khas.

The offspring of a Khas with a Magarin or Gurungin is a titular Khas, but his very father will not eat with him, nor any pure Khas.

The progeny of an Opadia Bráhman with a Thákúr woman, or a Thákúr with a Bráhman woman of Opadia class, gives a Hamál.

That of a Thákúr with a Magarin gives an Uchái Thákúr.

On the occasion of the birth of a child a rejoicing takes place for eleven days, and no one except near relatives can eat or drink with the father for ten days. On the eleventh day the Bráhman comes, performs certain ceremonies, after which the father is supposed to be clean, and all friends are feasted and alms are given. The same ceremony exactly takes place for a daughter as for a son, but the birth of the latter is hailed with joy, as he has to perform the "*Kiriya*" or funeral rites of the parents. The girl is looked upon more or less as an expense.

In our regiments eleven days' leave is always granted to a man when a child is born to him.

The Bráhman (Opadia) selects a name for the child on the eleventh day. Boys up to the age of 6 months, and girls up to 5 months, are allowed to suck their mothers' breasts only.

On arriving at that age a grand dinner is given, and the Bráhmans are feasted and propitiated.

Every friend and relation that has been invited is supposed to feed the child with grain, but this is merely a form, each man just putting a grain in the child's mouth.

The ceremony is called "*Bhát Khiláná*," "to feed with rice."

All the friends and relations are also supposed to give the child presents, which generally take the shape of bangles of silver or gold.

Betrothals (called *Mángni*) take place at any age over 5 years.

When a marriage is agreed upon, the parents of the boy give a gold ring to the girl, as a sign of betrothal.

This is called "*Sáhi Mundri*."

Five or six friends of the parents of the boy, and these must belong to the same clan as the boy, and five or six friends of the parents of the girl, and these must belong to the same clan as the girl's father, assemble to witness the agreement in the presence of a Bráhman.

A dinner is then given to the friends and relations of the contracting parties by the father of the girl, but the father of the boy is supposed to take with him some *dahi* (sour milk) and plantains as his share towards the dinner.

After a betrothal, except by breaking off the engagement, which can be done by going through a certain ceremony before witnesses, but which is considered very bad form, neither party can marry anyone else, unless on the death of one of them, when, if the real marriage has not taken place, or been consummated, they can do so.

Marriages can take place at any time after the age of 7. It is considered good to get a girl married before she reaches the age of 13.

A widow cannot marry a second time, but it is not considered disgraceful for her to form part of another man's household.

A widower can marry again.

If a boy, without being engaged to her, meets a girl, falls in love, runs away and marries her, he and his bride cannot approach the girl's father until called by him. When the father-in-law relents, he will send word telling the boy that he may present himself with his wife at his home on a certain hour of a certain day. On their arrival the father-in-law will paint a spot on their foreheads with a mixture of make submission. rice and *dahi* (*Tika Dinnu Garnu*;), and then the boy and girl will have to make submission by bending down and saluting him. This is called "*Dhok Dinnu.*"

Amongst Magars it is customary for marriages to be performed by Bráhmans, and the ceremony is conducted in much the same way as the ordinary Hindu marriage. There is the marriage ceremony *Jantí*, which is so timed as to reach the bride's house after midday, and which is first greeted with a shower of rice-balls, and then feasted by the parents of the bride. The actual marriage takes place at night, when the ceremony of Phera (circumambulation round the sacred fire) is performed, and afterwards the Anchal Ghátá (knotting a cloth which is stretched from the bridegroom's waist over the bride's shoulder).

The latter ceremony is said to constitute the essential marriage tie.

After marriage a divorce can be obtained by a Gurung (and often amongst Magars too) by going through a ceremony called "*Sinko Dágo*" or "*Sinko Pángrá*," but both the husband and wife must agree to this. A husband has to pay R40 for his divorce, and the wife R160. Two pieces of split *bambú* are tied together, placed on two mud balls, and the money is put close by. If either party takes up the *bambús*, breaks them, and picks up the money, the other party can go his or her way in peace and amity, and marry again legally.

In Népál, *Lámás*, assisted by *Giábrings*, fulfil the priestly functions of the Gurungs, both of the Chárját and the Soláhját, but in our regiments Gurung marriage ceremonies are performed by Bráhmans. They say with true philosophy, "*Jaisá Des Vaisá Bhes*," which might be translated as "*do in Rome as the Romans do.*"

In Népál, no ceremony, whether that of marriage, burial, or naming a child at birth, is performed until the officiating *Lámá* has determined the propitious moment by consultation of astrological tables, and by casting the horoscope. On this much stress is laid. In the marriage of Gurungs some ceremony resembling the Anchal Ghátá is performed by the *Lámás*, and red lead is sprinkled by the bridegroom over the head of the bride. This completes the actual ceremony. All friends and relations are supposed to look away from the bride whilst the red lead is actually being sprinkled. This ceremony is called "*Shindúr Hálnu*," "to sprinkle red lead."

A Magar will not allow his daughter to marry into the clan from which he may himself have taken a wife, but Gurungs have no objection to this. Neither Magars nor Gurungs, however, will take wives from the clan they may belong to themselves.

No Chárját Gurung can marry a Soláját or *vice versâ*.

In our regiments, on the death of a near relative, leave is granted for thirteen days. For a father the son mourns thirteen days. If an unmarried daughter dies, the father mourns thirteen days, unless she is still sucking her mother's breasts, when he would only mourn for five days. If a married daughter dies, the father mourns her for one day only, but the father-in-law will mourn for thirteen days.

Men shave their heads, lips, cheek, chins, and eyebrows for parents; also for an elder brother if both parents are dead, but not otherwise

Men only shave their heads for sons, younger brothers, and daughters if unmarried.

On the death of a Gurung in his own country he is buried. The following ceremony takes place. The body is wrapped round with many folds of white cloth, pinned together by splinters of wood; it is then carried by friends and relations to the grave-yard. At the entrance of the cemetery it is met by the officiating *Lámá*, who, dressed in a long white garment, walks round the cemetery, singing a *dirge*, and the body is carried behind him until he stops opposite the grave. It is next lowered into the grave, and then all friends and relations are supposed to throw a handful of earth upon the body, after which the grave is filled up, and stones placed above.

In our service Magars and Gurungs on death are either buried or burned (but nearly always buried), according to the wish of the nearest relative. If they die either of cholera or of smallpox, they are invariably buried.

Every regiment if possible should be provided with a cemetery. The men much appreciate this.

Magars and Gurungs are exceedingly superstitious. The most ordinary occurrences of every-day life are referred by them to supernatural agency, frequently to the malevolent action of some demon. These godlings have in consequence to be continually propitiated. Among the minor Hindu deities, Dioráli, Chandi, and Dévi are those specially worshipped in Goorkhá regiments. Outbreaks of any epidemic disease, such as cholera or smallpox, are invariably regarded as a malign visitation of Dioráli or Dévi. When going on a journey no one will start on an unlucky day of his own accord. After the date has been fixed, should any unforeseen occurrence prevent a man from starting, he will often walk out a mile or two on the road he intended taking, and leave a stick on the ground, as a proof of his intention having been carried out.

In March 1889 a Goorkhá woman died of cholera in the Gorakhpur recruiting *depôt*. Every Goorkhá officer, non-commissioned officer, and man at the *depôt*, at once subscribed. The recruiting officers gave their share, and with the proceeds three goats, three fowls, four pigeons, and food of sorts, were purchased. Of these one goat and the four pigeons were let loose, and the food thrown away in the name of Dévi, and the balance of animals were sacrificed to her, and then divided and eaten up. Before killing the animals, they all prayed together—"Oh, mother Dévi, we kill these beasts in thy name; do thou in return keep away all sickness from us."

As no fresh case occurred, although there was some cholera about in the district, all the Goorkhás in the *depôt* were more firmly convinced than ever that this was due entirely to their having propitiated Dévi.

Every Goorkhá regiment has a shrine to Deoráli, and on the seventh day of the Daséhrá this is visited by the whole battalion in state procession.

The following is a table of the festivals observed by Goorkhás in our service, with the leave allowed:—

Basant Panchmi (in honour of Spring)	1 day
Shibrátri	1 ,,
Holi (carnival)	9 days
Swan Sakráti	1 day
Riki Tarpan	1 ,,
Janam Asthmi (called Jaumasthami)	1 ,,
Dasehrá (called Dasain)	10 days.
Diwali (called Tiwár, the feast of lamps in honour of the Goddess Bhowini, at new moon of month of Kártik)	4 days
Máhia Sakrát (Hindu New Year)	1 day

The ceremonies at these festivals and their observance are, with a few minor points, the same as in Hindustán.

These holidays should not in any way be curtailed or interfered with, but should be granted in full.

The Daséhrá is the chief festival of the Goorkhás, and they endeavour to celebrate it whether in quarters or the field.

Great preparations are made for it in procuring goats, buffaloes, &c., for the sacrifice.

Every man in the regiment subscribes a certain amount towards the expenses. The commanding officers often give a buffaloe or two, and every British officer subscribes a certain amount also.

The arms of the regiment are piled, tents erected, and spectators invited to witness the dexterity of the men in severing the heads of buffaloes, the children performing the same office on goats. The period of this festival is considered an auspicious time for undertaking wars, expeditions, &c.

Caste rules with regard to food only apply to one description, viz.—"*dál* and rice."

All other food, excepting "*dál* and rice," *all* Goorkhás will eat in common.

With Magars, unmarried Thákúrs, and with Gurungs, it is not necessary to take off any clothes to cook or to eat any kind of food, including "*dál* and rice."

In Népál the Khas need only remove their caps and shoes to cook or eat their food.

Should a Bráhman of the Opadia class prepare "*dál* and rice," all castes can eat of it.

Magars and Gurungs will not eat the above if prepared by a Jaici Bráhman.

Superior castes will not eat *dál* and rice with inferior ones. In our regiments men generally form little messes of their own varying in size from two or three to a dozen.

As long as they are unmarried, Goorkhás of the same caste will eat everything together.

All Goorkhás will eat "*shikar*" in common, a word they use for all descriptions of meat.

No Goorkhás, except some menial classes, will eat cows, *neilgai*, or female goats.

Gurungs eat buffaloes in their own country, though they will stoutly deny it if accused.

All kinds of game are prized by Goorkhás, deer of all varieties, pigs, porcupines, pea-fowl, pigeons, pheasants, &c., &c., but beyond all things a Goorkhá likes fish.

Whilst bachelors, Magars and Gurungs will eat every kind of food in common, and after marriage even, the only thing they draw the line at, is "*dál* and rice."

Food cooked in *ghee*, including "rice," but not "*dál*," is eaten by all classes in common.

Thákúrs who have not adopted the thread will eat everything with Magar and Gurung.

All classes will drink water from the same *masak*, which, however, should be made of goat-skin,

Brian Hodgson gives the following true and graphic account of the contrast between the way the Goorkhá eats his food and the preliminary ceremonies which have to be observed by the orthodox Hindu:—

> These highland soldiers, who despatch their meal in half an hour, and satisfy the ceremonial law by merely washing their hands and face and taking off their turbans before cooking, laugh at the pharisaical rigour of the *Sipáhis*, who must bathe from head to foot, and make *puja* ere they can begin to dress, their dinners must eat nearly naked in the coldest weather, and cannot be in marching trim again in less than three hours.
>
> In war, the former readily carry several days' provisions on their backs: the latter would deem such an act intolerably degrading. The former see in foreign service nothing but the prospect of

glory and spoil: the latter can discover in it nothing but pollution and peril from unclean men and terrible wizards, goblins, and evil spirits. In masses the former have all that indomitable confidence, each in all, which grows out of national integrity and success: the latter can have no idea of this sentiment, which yet maintains the union and resolution of multitudes in peril better than all other human bonds whatsoever, and once thoroughly acquired, is by no means inseperable from service under the national standard.

In my humble opinion they are by far the best soldiers in Asia; and if they were made participators of our renown in arms, I conceive that their gallant spirit, emphatic contempt of *madhesias* (people residing in the plains), and unadulterated military habits, might be relied on for fidelity; and that our good and regular pay and noble pension establishment would serve perfectly to counterpose the influence of nationality so far as that could injuriously affect us.

The above was written by Mr. Brian Hodgson in 1832, and 25 years later, namely, in 1857, he writes:—

It is infinitely to be regretted that the opinions of Sir H. Fane, of Sir Charles Napier, and of Sir H. Lawrence, as to the high expediency of recruiting largely from this source, were not acted upon long ago.

On service the Goorkhás put aside the very small caste prejudices they have, and will cook and eat their food, if necessary, in uniform, and with all accoutrements on.

Goorkhás will eat all and every kind of vegetables and fruit. They have a great partiality for garlic and pepper, and are very fond of potatoes, cabbages, cucumbers, and squash (*kadu*). Goorkhás will drink any English spirits, wines, or beer.

They manufacture a kind of beer out of rice, which they call *Jánr*, and a spirit called *Raksi*, and although they will drink this freely, they far prefer good Commissariat rum.

They will smoke any English or Indian tobacco, and are very fond of *cheroots*.

They will smoke out of any English-made pipe, even if with a horn mouth-piece, although they are likely to make a little fuss over the latter, just to save their consciences.

The *kukri*, a short, curved, broad-bladed, and heavy knife, is the real national weapon of the Goorkhás, and it is worn by all from the highest to the lowest. In our regiments they are carried in a *frog* attached to the waist-belt.

From the beginning of the handle to the end or point of the blade they average about 20 inches in length.

Where wood is plentiful, they are very fond of practising cutting with the *kukri*, and they will cut down with one blow a tree the size of an ordinary man's arm.

A really skilful cutter will cut off slice after slice from the cud of a piece of green wood, each slice being not thicker than an ordinary piece of shoe leather. They call this *"chinnu"* "to slice off."

They are also skilful with the *Golel*, knocking down and killing the smallest birds with ease. All who can manage to raise the funds endeavour to possess themselves of some sort of firearm.

The national dress of the Goorkhás of the poorer class, such as we enlist, is one that shows them off to the greatest advantage, and consists of the following:—

A piece of cloth (*langote*) worn, as natives of India do, round the loins, &c.

A thin waistcoat fitting tight and buttoned all the way up to the throat,

A long piece of cloth, which is often a *pagri*, and is wrapped round the waist, and by which the *kukri* is carried.

A pair of brown Goorkhá shoes, as described further on.

A black round cap, high on one side and low on the other, and finally a kind of thin blanket or thick sheet, called *Khádi*, which is worn as follows:—

The two corners of the breadth are first taken. One is carried over the right shoulder and the other is brought up under the left arm, and the two corners tied together about the centre of the chest.

A third corner, the one diagonally opposite No.1, is now taken, and brought over the left shoulder and tied in a knot with the fourth corner, which is brought up under the right arm and opposite the centre of the chest.

This dress leaves the arms quite bare from above the elbows, and the legs are naked from halfway down to the knees, thus showing off his grand limbs.

The blanket, by being tied as described above, forms a kind of large bag, which extends all the way round the back, and in this Goorkhás very often carry their goods and chattels.

The Goorkhá shoe is square-toed, fits well up over the instep, passes just under the ankle, and then round and pretty high up above the heel. It is made of rough looking but good brown leather, and all sewing in it is done with strips of raw hide.

It is an excellent, durable shoe, is not affected by water in the same way that an ordinary native shoe of India is, and it is much less liable to come off in boggy ground.

When the sun is very hot, Goorkhás will often unwind their waist-belt and tie the same over their heads in the shape of a *pagri*, taking it off again in the afternoon, when it begins to cool down again.

The upper classes of Népál and most of the residents of Katmandu wear the following:—

The abovementioned national cap, or one much like it.

A kind of double-breasted frock coat called *chaubandi*, fitting tight everywhere, especially over the arms, and fastened inside and outside by means of eight pieces of coloured tape, four inside and four outside. The four outside pieces of tape when tied show two on the left breast and high up, and the other two on the left side about level with the waist.

A white or coloured waist cloth or *págri*, with the invariable *kukri*, a pair of *pyjámas* very loose down to just below the knee, and from thence fitting the leg down to the ankle, and a pair of the national shoes.

Under the coat is worn a shirt, of which three or four inches are invariably allowed to show. They never tuck their shirts inside their *pyjámas*.

The frock coat and *pyjáma* abovementioned are made of a double layer of a thin shiny cotton cloth. Between the two layers a padding of cotton wool is placed, and these secured by parallel lines of sewing, which run close to each other.

To make this still more secure, diagonal lines of sewing are also resorted to. This makes a very comfortable, and warm, but light suit.

Goorkhás delight in all manly sports,—shooting, fishing, &c.—and are mostly keen sportsmen and possess sports. great skill with gun and rod. They amuse themselves in their leisure hours, either in this way in the field, or in putting the shot, playing quoits or football, and they are always eager to join in any game with Europeans.

General Sir Charles Reid, K.C.B., says—

All Goorkhás are keen sportsmen, and are never so happy as

when they are on a tiger's track. A man I lost at Delhi had killed twenty-two on foot; they never waste a shot; they call ammunition '*Khazána*,' 'treasure.'

They are good gardeners, but very improvident, as they never will save up seed for the next season's sowing.

They are very fond of flowers, and will often go a long distance to procure some. They often make necklaces of flowers, which they wear, and will also put flowers away in a glass of water in their barracks.

As compared with other Orientals, Goorkhás are bold, enduring, faithful, frank, very independent and self-reliant; in their own country they are jealous of foreigners and self-asserting.

They despise the natives of India, and look up to and fraternize with Europeans, whom they admire for their superior knowledge, strength and courage, and whom they imitate in dress and habits.

They have the following saying "*Topiwár Kámwár, Lungiwár Khánnewár*"—"The cap wearer works, the *lungi*-wearer eats."

They are very jealous of their women, but are domestic in their habits, and kind and affectionate husbands and parents.

As a consequence their wives are less shy and reserved, and have more freedom, and reciprocate their affection, carefully looking after uniform and all culinary and domestic matters.

As a rule recruits on joining are very unsophisticated, very truthful, but dirty, and the first lesson that has to be taught them is that "cleanliness is next to godliness." They have then few prejudices of any description, caste or otherwise.

The great vice of Goorkhás is gambling, to which they are greatly addicted. Though hot-tempered and easily roused, they are in general quiet, well-behaved men, and extremely amenable to discipline. With a firm just hand over them, punishments are rare.

Goorkhás are capable of being polished up to a degree of smartness that no native troops can approach, and which cannot be much surpassed even by British troops.

No officer can be too strict with them in parades, but they hate being "nagged at."

With a slack hand over them they very soon deteriorate and become slovenly.

In Katmandu good schools exist in which English and Hindi are taught, but our recruits, being almost entirely drawn from the agricultural classes, are quite ignorant of reading or writing.

In our battalions schools exist for their instruction in reading, writing, and doing accounts, both in English and vernacular, and these are generally well attended. Numbers of men learn to read and write from friends in their barracks.

It may seem strange, but it is an undoubted fact, that a number of recruits are yearly obtained who profess to enlist merely for the sake of learning to read, write, and do accounts.

The Goorkhá, from the warlike qualities of his forefathers, and the traditions handed down to him of their military prowess as conquerors of Népál, is imbued with, and cherishes, the true military spirit.

His physique, compact and sturdy build, powerful muscular development, keen sight, acute hearing, and hereditary education as a sportsman, eminently capacitate him for the duties of a light infantry soldier on the mountain side, while his acquaintance with forest lore makes him as a pioneer in a jungle almost unrivalled, whilst his national weapon the *kukri* has in Burmah and other places proved itself invaluable.

The bravery displayed by the Goorkhás in their contests with the British has already been alluded to, and their own traditions afford ample proof of the dogged tenacity with which they can encounter danger and hardship.

The return of the Népál army from Diggarcheh in the year 1790, amongst other instances, affords a distinguished proof of their daring and hardihood. The following extracts from Captain T. Smith's book are very characteristic.

> At Bhartpur it was an interesting and amusing sight to witness the extreme good-fellowship and kindly feeling with which the Europeans and the Goorkhás mutually regarded each other. A six-foot-two grenadier of the 59th would offer a *cheroot* to the "little Goorkhee," as he styled him; the latter would take it from him with a grin, and when his tall and patronising comrade stooped down with a lighted cigar in his mouth, the little mountaineer never hesitated a moment in puffing away at it with the one just received, and they were consequently patted on the back and called "prime chaps."
>
> At the assault of Bhartpur, the Goorkhás were ordered to follow in after the 59th.
>
> These directions were obeyed, with the exception of going in with them instead of after them; for when the British grena-

diers with a deafening "hurrah" made their maddening rush at the breach, at that glorious and soul-stirring moment it was impossible to restrain them, and they dashed into the thick of it. In the morning after the storming of Bhartpur, when being praised for their gallantry by their British comrades, they returned the flattering partiality of the latter by the following characteristic remark: "The English are brave as lions; they are splendid *sepoys*, and *very nearly* equal to us!"

The following story is given as illustrative of their coolness and amenability to discipline.

A tiger had been seen within a few miles of Dehra, and Colonel Young (then captain, and the gallant commanding officer of the Simcor battalion), accompanied by Colonel Childers of Her Majesty's 11th Dragoons, mounted an elephant and hastened to the spot. They, however, were unsuccessful in rousing him; and after a long and tedious search were returning home.

A Goorkhá *sepoy* was following the elephant with his gun on his shoulder, when he suddenly dropped on one knee and presented his rifle as if in the act to fire. Having, however, roused the attention of the sportsmen, he did not pull the trigger but kept his gun fixed in the same position. He had suddenly caught sight of the fiery eyes of the tiger, who was crouching amongst the underwood, within three paces of his gun; in this situation they steadily regarded each other. The elephant was immediately pushed up close to the kneeling Goorkhá, but neither of the sportsmen could succeed in catching a glimpse of the animal. In order, if possible, to observe the direction more accurately, Captain Young called out "Recover arms." The *sepoy* came to the "Recover" as calmly and collectedly as if on his own parade. "Present." Down went the gun again; this was repeated, but still the tiger was invisible.

Captain Young exclaimed "That gallant fellow shall not be left unassisted," and in a moment dropped from the elephant and placed himself close to the *sepoy*. He looked along the levelled barrel, but to no purpose; the brute was not to be distinguished.

Cocking his gun, therefore, he told the Goorkhá to fire; there was a terrific roar, a rush forward for one instant, and all was still. When the smoke had just cleared away, there lay the tiger perfectly dead. The ball had struck the centre of his forehead and entered his brain.

Doctor Oldfield in his book points out that there is not a single instance of a Nepál chief taking bribes from, or selling himself for money to, the British or any other state. This loyalty to themselves is only equalled by their loyalty to us during the fiery ordeal of the Mutiny, the records of which, as well as of Ambela, of the Cabul campaign, and many other wars and battles, amply testify the value of the services rendered us by our Goorkhá regiments since incorporation in our army in 1815.

Their fighting qualities, whether for sturdy, unflinching courage, or daring *élan*, are *"nulli secundus"* amongst the troops we enrol in our ranks from the varied classes of our Indian Empire, and no greater compliment can be paid to their bravery than by quoting one of their sayings—

Káfar hunnu bhandá, manrnu rámro!
It is better to die than to be a coward!

PART 4

Tribes, Clans, &c.

Remarks on Goorkhá Tribes and Clans.

The military tribes of Népál, from which the fighting element is almost exclusively drawn, are the following:—

The Khas, Magar, Gurung, and Thákúr.

There are also a few Limbús and Rais to be found in most of our Goorkhá regiments, but they are very few in number and only very slight mention is made of them in this book, as they are residents of Eastern and North-Eastern Népál, and are hardly ever brought in for enlistment to the recruiting officer at Gorakhpur.

A few Nagarkotis (*Newars*) are also found in most of the regiments.

KHAS

The Khas are the predominant race of Népál. They are generally slighter, more active, and more intelligent, than either the Magar or Gurung.

They are Hindús, wear the thread, and are more liable to Bráhmanical prejudices than the Magar or Gurung. They, however, make little of the ceremonial law of the Hindus in regard to food and sexual relations. Their active habits and vigorous characters could not brook the restraint of ritual law. Their few prejudices are rather useful than otherwise, inasmuch as they favour sobriety and cleanliness.

They are temperate, hardy and brave, and make good soldiers. They intermarry in their own castes, and have a high social standing in Népál.

In the Népálese army almost all the officers above the rank of lieutenant are Khas, and so are by far the greater proportion of officers below the rank of captain.

They are intensely proud of their traditions, and look down upon

Magars and Gurungs.

In their own country any Khas who runs away in a battle becomes an outcast, and his very wife is unable to eat with him. They are very national in their feelings.

In the Népálese "Rifle Brigade," which consists of the picked men of all classes, are to be found numbers of Khas of 5' 9" and over, with magnificent physique.

Colonel Bahádar Gambar Sing, who at present commands the "Rifles," served as a private under Sir Jang Bahádar at Lucknow during the Mutiny. He there greatly distinguished himself by single-handed capturing three guns and killing seven mutineers. He received an acknowledgment from the British Government for his bravery, and the Prince of Wales presented him in 1875 with a claymore, with an inscription thereon. In this fight Colonel Gambar Sing had no other weapon than his *kukri*, and he received 23 wounds, some of which were very dangerous, and to this day his face is scarred with huge sword-cuts. He also lost some fingers, and one of his hands was nearly cut off. Sir Jang Bahádar had a special medal struck for him, which the gallant old gentleman wears on all great parades.

None of our Goorkhá regiments enlist Khas now, although in most regiments a few are to be still found, who were enlisted in olden days.

Experience would seem to prove that Magars and Gurungs are undoubtedly better men than Khas, yet a regiment of Khas would make a very fine body of soldiers, and in the present days, when men of good fighting class are so much needed, it seems a pity that Government makes no use of this material, out of which a regiment or two could easily be raised.

About Khattris, Dr. L. Hamilton says:—

> The descendants of Bráhmans by women of the lower tribes, although admitted to be Khas (or impure), are called *Kshattris* or *Khattris*, which terms are considered as perfectly synonymous.

> It would seem, however, that some proper *Khattris*, called "*Deokotas*," from Bareilly, did settle in the country, and intermarried with the Khas *Khattris*, All the *Khattris* wear the thread, and are considered as belonging to the military tribes.

> Since the return of Jang Bahádar from England, a number of Goorkhá Khas have taken to calling themselves *Chattris*. There is no

such man in the whole of Népál as a Goorkhá *Chattri.*

Khas there are and *Khattris* there are also, but *Chattris* there are none, and it is merely a title borrowed latterly from India.

Brian Hodgson also mentions a tribe called Ekthariahs, the descendants of more or less pure Rájpúts and other Kshatriyas of the plains. They claimed a vague superiority to the Khas, but the great tide of events around them has now thoroughly confounded the two races in all essentials, and therefore they will not be shown as a separate tribe, but be included with Khas. Brian Hodgson says:—

> The Khas were, long previously to the age of Prithvi Narayan, extensively spread over the whole of the Cháubisia, and they are now to be found in every part of the existing kingdom of Népál, as well as in Kumáon, which was part of Népál until 1816. The Khas are more devoted to the house of Goorkhá, as well as more liable to Bráhmanical prejudices, than the Magars or Gurungs; and on both accounts are perhaps somewhat less desirable as soldiers for our service than the latter tribes.[1] I say somewhat, because it is a mere question of degree; the Khas having certainly no religious prejudices, nor probably any national partialities which would prevent their making excellent and faithful servants-in-arms; and they possess pre-eminently that masculine energy of character and love of enterprise which distinguish so advantageously all the military races of Népál.

For the origin of the Khas nation, see under heading of "History."

To the north and to the west of Sallián, numbers of Matwala Khas are to be found. They are rarely if ever found to the east of the Gandak River. There can be no doubt that this race found its origin somewhere about Sallián, or perhaps still further west.

The Matwala Khas is generally the progeny of a Khas of Western Népál with a Magar woman of Western Népál.

If the woman happens to belong to the Ráná clan of the Magar tribe, the progeny is then called a Bhát Ráná.

The Matwala Khas does not wear the thread. He eats and drinks, and in every way assimilates himself with the Magars and Gurungs. He invariably claims to be a Magar.

Amongst the Matwala Khas are to be found those who call them-

---

1. This was written in 1832,—namely, only sixteen years after our war with Népál —and it is on that account that Brian Hodgson says the Khas are somewhat less desirable as soldiers for our service—not for want of bravery or soldierly qualities.

selves Bohra, Roká, Chohán, Jhánkri, &c.

These are easy to identify, but it is more difficult to find out a Matwala who calls himself a Thápá. His strong Magar appearance, his not wearing the thread, and his eating and drinking freely with the real Magars, all tend to prove him to be what he almost invariably claims to be, *viz.*, a real Magar. The writer has found men in the ranks who for years had served as, and been considered, Magars, but who really were Matwala Khas. Some very excellent recruits are obtained amongst the Matwala Khas, although the greater proportion are coarse-bred and undesirable.

KHAS.

Adikhári Clans.

Dhámi.	Pokriál.
Khadsena.	Thákúri.
Man.	Thámi.
Musiah.	Tharirái.

Baniah Clans.
Sinjapati.

Basnáyet Clans.

Khaptari.	Rakmi.
Khúlál.	Sripáli.
Puwár.	

Bhandári Clans.

Lámá.	Sinjápati.
Raghúbangsi.	

Bhist Clans.

Dahál.	Puwár.
Kálikotia.	

Gharti Clans.

Kálikotia.	Khánka.
Bagália.	Khúlál.

Kárkhi Clans.

Khúlál.	Mundala.
Lámá.	Sutar.

Khánka Clans.

Kálikotia.	Mahárájí.
Khaptari.	Palpáli.
Khúlál.	Partiál.
Lakángi.	Powar.

Lámchania.

Khattri Clans (progeny mostly of Jaici or Bráhmans with Khas).

Adikhári.	Khúlál.
Arjál.	Kirkiseni.
Barál.	Lámchania.
Bhatári.	Pánde.
Bhúsál.	Panth.
Dál.	Parajuli.
Dangáli.	Phaniá
Deokota.	Poryál.
Dhakál.	Remi.
Dhamál.	Sakhtiál.
Ditál.	Sápkotia.
Ghimiria.	Silwal.
Gothami.	Suveri.
Khaptari.	Tewári.

Kanwár Clans.

Arjál.	Khánka.
Bagália.	Khúlál.

Thápá Clans.

Bagiál.	Maháráji.
Deoga.	Palámi.
Gagliyá.	Parájuli.
Ghimiria.	Puwár.
Gudár.	Saniál.
Khaptari.	Súyál.
Khúlál.	Thákuriál.
Lámchania.	

Other true Khas but not classified yet.

Alpháltopi.	Batiál.
Am Gái.	Bhát Ojha.
Baj Gái.	Bhát Rai.
Balia.	Bhirial.
Bámankoti.	Bikrál.
Chalatáni.	Lamsál.
Chanial.	Mari Bhús.
Chanvala Gái.	Naopánia.
Dahal.	Osti.
Danjal.	Parijai Kawale.
Deokota (Khattri).	Parsái.
Dhongial.	Pauriál.
Dhungána.	Porseni.

Ganjál.	Pungiál.
Gartola.	Regmi (Khattri).
Gilal.	Rúpakheti.
Hamia Gái.	Satania.
Kadariah.	Sáti.
Kálá Khattri.	Satia Gái.
Kanhal.	Seora.
Khatiwata.	Sikhimial.
Kilathani.	Sijal.
Kukriál.	Tewári (Khattri).
Layál.	Túmrakal.

MAGARS AND GURUNGS.

These are by common consent recognised as the *beau ideal* of what a Goorkhá soldier should be.

As these tribes have submitted to the ceremonial law of purity and to Bráhmanical supremacy, they have been adopted as Hindus, but they have been denied the sacred thread, and take rank as a doubtful order below the Kshatriya.

They are practically only Hindús because it is the fashion; they have gone with the times, and consequently their Hinduism is not very strict, and they are decidedly the least prejudiced in caste matters of all classes of Népál who seek our service. They participated in all the military successes of the house of Goorkhá., and although they have less sympathy with the Government, they are still very loyal to it.

The Gurungs lent themselves less early, and less heartily, to Bráhmanical influences, and they have retained to a greater extent than the Magars their national peculiarities and language. In stature the Gurungs are generally larger and more powerful than the Magars and Khas.

The Magars and Gurungs have already been referred to as being of the Tartar race; they in Népál follow agricultural pursuits; they are square-built, sturdy men, with fine muscular, and large chest and limb development, low in stature, and with little or no hair on face or body, and with fair complexions. They are a merry-hearted race, eat animal food, and in Népál drink a kind of beer made from rice called *janr* and a kind of spirit called *raksi*. In our battalions they will drink any English wine, spirits, or beer. They are intensely fond of soldiering.

They are very hardy and extremely simple-minded. They are kind-hearted and generous, and as recruits absolutely truthful. They are very proud and sensitive, and they deeply feel abuse or undeserved censure. They are very obstinate, very independent, very vain, and in their plain clothes inclined to be dirty. They are intensely loyal to each other and their officers in time of trouble or danger.

Brian Hodgson says about Magars and Gurungs:—

From lending themselves less early and heartily to Bráhmanical influences than the Khas, they have retained, in vivid freshness, their original languages, physiognomy, and, in a less degree, habits. Their two languages differ materially, though both belonging to the unpronominalised type of the Turanian tongues.

The Gurungs are less generally and more recently redeemed from Lámáism and primitive impurity than the Magars.

But though both the Gurungs and Magars still retain their own vernacular tongues, Tartar faces, and careless manners, yet, what with military service for several generations under the predominant Khas, and what with the commerce of Khas males with their females, they have acquired the Khas language, though not to the oblivion of their own, and the Khas habits and sentiments, but with sundry reservations in favour with pristine liberty.

As, however, they have, with such grace as they could muster, submitted themselves to the ceremonial laws of purity, and to Bráhman supremacy, they have been adopted as Hindús, but they have been denied the thread, and constitute a doubtful order below it.

The Gurung tribe consists of two great divisions—

1. The Chárját.
2. The Soláhját.

The Chárját, as its name implies, is composed of four castes, *viz*.:—

1. Ghallea. ,
2. Ghotáni (sometimes Ghundani).
3. Lámá.
4. Lámchania.

Each of these four castes comprises a number of clans, and some of these are again subdivided into families.

The Chárját Gurung might be called the Gurung nobility.

Every Gurung recruit knows perfectly well whether he belongs to the Chárját or to the Soláhját, but numbers of the latter will try to claim the former. A little trouble will almost invariably bring out the truth.

The Chárját Gurung is very much looked up to by the Soláhját.

A Soláhját Gurung cannot marry a Chárját, nor can he ever by any means become a Chárját.

Questioning a Chárját Gurung would be much as follows;—

"What is your name?" "Jasbir Gurung."
"What Gurung are you?" "Chárját."
"Which of the Chárját?" "Lámchania."
"Which Lámchania clan?" "Plohnian."
"What Plohnian?" "Átbai."

Of the Chárját Gurungs the Ghallea is by far the most difficult to obtain.

The Plohnian and Chenwári clans of the Lámchania are both subdivided into families; the best Plohnian family is the Átbai, and the best of the Chenwári is the Chárghari.

It will be noticed that nearly all Ghotani clans end with "ron."

Some excellent recruits are also obtained from the Soláhját.

Traditions

In olden days the Ghalleas ruled the country about Lámzúng and had their own king, a Ghallea.

Their kingdom nominally exists to this day, (at time of first publication).

The following tradition regarding the birth of the Chárját exists:—

A Thákúr king asked the king of Lámzúng for his daughter's hand in marriage.

The Ghallea king accepted the proposal favourably, and sent a young and beautiful maiden as his daughter to the Thákúr king, who duly married her, and by her begot several children.

Some years afterwards it transpired that this young maiden was no king's daughter, but merely one of her slave attendants; whereupon the Thákúr king was very angry, and sent a message threatening war, unless the Ghallea king sent him his real daughter.

The king of Lámzúng thereupon complied, and this time sent his real daughter, whom the Thákúr king married, and by whom he begot three sons. (From these three sons are descended the Ghotáni,

Lámá, and Lámchania clans.)

It was then ruled that these three sons and their descendants should rank equal to the Ghallea clan, and that they should be called the Chárját Gurungs, whilst the descendants of the children of the slave-mother should be called Soláhjáts and should forever be servants to the Chárját.

From this it would appear that the Ghallea Gurung is the oldest and the purest of all Gurung clans. They certainly are splendid men of the purest Goorkhá type.

The Gurungs have for centuries kept up their history, which is called in Khaskúra "*Gurung ko Bangsáoli.*"

When the famous case of Colonel Lachman Gurung took place, Sir Jang Bahádar, being anxious to elucidate, if possible, the difference between Chárját and Soláhját Gurungs, had the history of the Gurungs brought to him, and having read the same, declared that the Soláhját Gurungmust remain satisfied with his present position, and be forever the servant of the Chárját.

The Soláhját Gurung will always make obeisance to the Chárját, and when travelling in their own country, the Soláhját will generally carry the Chárját's load.

It is said that Colonel Lachman Gurung offered his daughter's weight in gold to any Chárját who would marry her. A poor man of the Ghotáni clan, being sorely tempted by the bribe, offered himself as a husband, but was at once outcasted and reduced to a Soláhját, and so the marriage never came off.

Many centuries ago, it is said, a landslip occurred which buried a whole village, and destroyed all the inhabitants, except one small boy, who was found by a Lámchania Gurung amongst the *débris*.

He took the boy home and adopted him, but as he did not know who the father of the boy was, a difficulty arose in time as to what clan this boy should belong to.

The Lámás, on being consulted, ruled that the child and all his descendants should be called Tutia Lámchanias (*Tutia* means broken, rugged), because he had been found on broken, rugged ground.

A boy that had been deserted was found by a Lámchania Gurung amongst some reeds. It was settled that this boy and all his descendants should be called Plohnian Lámchanias (*Plohn* means reeds), because he had been found amongst reeds.

There are two regiments of Gurungs in the Népálese army—the Káli Bahádar and the Káli Persad. The former is absolutely a Gurung regiment, and most of the men are Chárját Gurungs. They are a magnificent body of men, consisting of all the picked Gurungs of Nepál. They must average over 5' 6" in height, with splendid physique.

GURUNGS.

Ghallea Clans (Chárját).

Gerlen	(excellent).	Sámri	(excellent).
*Gyapsing	?	Samunder	(good.)
*Pyling	?	*Sinjáli	?
*{ Rájvansi or Rájbangsi	?	*{ Súrjabansi or Súrajvánsi.	?
Rilten	(excellent).		

* I doubt the existence of these five clans as pure Ghalleas. The only four that I know as real Ghalleas are the Rilten, Sámri, Gerlen, and Samunder, of which the first three are the best. I have never seen a single case of a Súrjabansi Gurung, nor do I believe in their existence, after careful enquiry.—E. V.

Ghotáni Clans (Chárját).

Adunron.	Migiron.
Chomron.	Nagiron.
Gholron.	Náikron.
Kaliron.	Pochkiron.
Kamjai.	Rijoron.
Kelonron.	Tagren.
Kongron.	Thákúron.
Kudlron.	Tenron.
Mazuron.	Walron.

Lámá Clans (Chárját).

Chelen.	Púngi.
Chenwári.	Tengi.
Khimu.	Tidún or Titún.
Kurúngi.	Timji.
Nakchia.	Tonder.
Pengi.	Urdúng.
Phache (pronounced Fache).	

Lámchania Clans (Chárját).

Adi.	Naikron.
Chen } probably the	Pajji Lem.*
Chenwári } same.	Pángi.
Kaliron.	Plitti.
Kroko Lem.*	Plohnian.
Kurbu { ? Doubtful; perhaps Soláhját.	Púrani.
	Silangi.
Lem.	Tutia } probably the
Lengra.	Twidian } same.
Marenu.	

* Kroko Lem and Pajji Lem are both the same, but the former is in Gurung Khura, the latter in Khas Khura.—E. V.

GURUNGS OF THE SOLAHJAT.

Allea.†
Bhúj or Bhújia.
Chágli.
Chime.
Chohomonú.
Chormi.
Chornú.
Darlámi ‡
Diál.
Dingiál.
Ghabbú.
Ghorenj.
Gnór.
Gúlángiá.
Giábring.
Húrdún.
Timali.
Tumreh.

Kepchen.
Khaptari.
Khatrain.
Khúlál.
Kinjú.
Kokiá.
Kongi Lámá.
Kúmái.
Kromjái.
Kiápchain.
Láhor.
Leghen.
Lohan (probably Láhor).
Lyúng
Main.
Mapchain.
Masrági.
Mobjai (or Mahbrijai).

† This is the Khas Khura name for a clan. I have forgotten the Gurung Khura name.
—E. V.
‡ This perhaps should be spelt Darra Lámi.—E. V.

Mor (or Mormain).
Murum.
Nanra.
Nánsing.
Pajju.
Pálná.
Phíwáli { (or Piwáli or Phiúyáli).
Plén.
Ploplo.
Pomái.
Ponjú.
Rilah.
Rimália.

Sárbújá.
Tahin.
Takrain.
Táme.
Telej.
Tendúr.
Tenlájá.
Thár.
Tingi Lámá.
Tol.
Tolangi.
Torjain.
Úzc.

MAGARS.

The Magars are divided into six distinct tribes, and no more, although the following all claim to be Magars and try in every way to establish themselves as such:—

Bohra (really a Matwala Khas of Western Népál)
Roka. (ditto   ditto   ditto).
Chohán (ditto   ditto   ditto).
Jhánkri (ditto   ditto   ditto).

Konwár (progeny of mendicant).
Úchái (*ditto* Thákúr).

In days of old a certain number of Magars were driven out of their own country, and settled in Western Népál amongst strangers. From the progeny of these sprang up many clans of mixed breeds, who now claim to be purebred Magars, but are not recognised as such.

In addition to the few mentioned above, are some others who also claim to be Magars, such as Rawats, Dishwas, &c., but as they have no real relationship to Magars, it is considered unnecessary to enter a list of them here.

The real and only Magars are divided into the following six tribes, which are here entered alphabetically :—

1. Allea.
2. Búrathoki.
3. Gharti.
4. Pún.
5. Ráná.
6. Thápá.

These tribes all intermarry with each other, have the same customs and habits, and are in every way equal as regards social standing, with perhaps a slight preference in favour of the Rind.

The original home of the Magars was to the west of the Gandak River (Káli-wár[1]), and, roughly speaking, consisted of that portion of Népál which lies between and round about Gúlmi, Argha, Kháchi, and Pálpá.

This bit of country was divided into twelve districts (Báráh Mangránth[2]), and the residents of the same in time came to be spoken of as the Magars of the Báráh Mangránth.

Brian Hodgson and Captain T. Smith both give the following as the Báráh Mangránth:—Satúng, Pyúng, Bhirkot, Dhor, Garhúng, Rising, Ghiring, Gúlmi, Argha, Kháchi, Musikot, and Isma.

By the term "Báráh Mangránth Magars" no particular set of tribes was meant. The term had a purely local meaning, and referred to all such Magars, of whatever tribe they might be, whose ancestors had

---

1. Dr. Hamilton in his book published in 1819 says:—"Before the arrival of the Rájpúts, it is said that the Magar nation consisted of twelve Tháms, the whole members of each being supposed to have a common extraction in the male line. Each Thám was governed by a chief, considered as the head of a common family."—E.V.
2. The Sardáh on the west and the Gandak in the centre of Népál are both spoken of as the Káli.—E.V.

resided for generations within the Báráh Mangránth.

Each of these twelve districts had its own ruler, but it would appear that the most powerful kings were those of Gúlmi, Argha, Kháchi, and that the remaining princes were more or less tributary to these three.

Since the rise of the house of Goorkhá, towards the close of the eighteenth century, the country has been redivided, and the twelve districts no longer exist as such, and the term "*Báráh Mangránth Magar*" has no signification now, and is therefore falling into disuse. Not one recruit out of fifty knows what the term means.

As mentioned before, the original home of the Magars was to the west of the Gandak River, but it would seem that some clans had for ages occupied certain portions of Népál on the east bank.

The city of Goorkhá was originally the residence of the Chitoriáh Ránás. It is supposed the city was built by them, and to this day numbers of Chitoriáh Ránás are found there.

The Magars having participated in the military conquests of the house of Goorkhá, spread themselves far and wide all over Népál, and numbers are now to be found to the east of the Gandak River.

The Alleas in appearance seem a very pure bred race. As a rule they are very fair, well-made men. The Allea tribe must, however, be rather a small one, as the percentage of Alleas enlisted yearly is very small. They are most desirable men to get.

Búrathokis are also apparently very limited in number. Some excellent specimens of Goorkhás are, however, every year obtained from this tribe. They are very desirable men to get.

The Ghartis are pretty numerous, but care should be taken in enlisting from this tribe, as they seem to be far more mixed than any of the other five pure Magar tribes. By careful selection, however, excellent Ghartis can be obtained.

The Bhújiál Gharti lives in the valleys and high mountains to the north of Gúlmi, above the Puns, but immediately below the Karántis. Their tract of country runs along both sides of the Bhúji Khola (river), from which they probably derive their name.

The Bhújial Gharti is generally a shepherd. He lives principally on the milk of sheep, and is almost invariably a man of very good physique and heavy limbs. He is remarkably dirty when first enlisted.

Amongst the Gharti clans are two that should not be confounded, although from their similarity in pronunciation one is very apt to do so. The Paháre or Pahária is a good Magar. The Páre or Pária (from *par*, outside) should never be enlisted. He is, as his name indicates, an outcaste, or a descendant of outcastes.

The Pún tribe seems a small one, as but a small percentage of them is obtained annually. They are generally men of heavy limbs and excellent physique. They much resemble Gurungs. They live about Gúlmi principally, although of course they are found in other places also. They are most desirable men.

Of all Magars there is no better man than a Ráná of good clan. In former days any Thápá who had lost three generations of ancestors in battle became a Ráná, but with the prefix of his Thápá clan. Thus a Reshmi Thápá would become a Reshmi Ráná.

An instance of this is to be found in the 5th Goorkhás, where a *havildar*, Lachman Thápá, and a *naick*, Shamsher Ráná, are descended from two Thápá brothers; but three generations of descendants from one of these brothers having been killed in battle, Shamsher Ráná's ancestors assumed the title of Ráná; Lachman Thápá's ancestors not having been killed in battle for three generations, he remains a Thápá.

From this custom many Ráná clans are said to have sprung up, and this would lead one to believe that the Ráná tribe was looked up to amongst Magars.

The original Ráná clans were few, amongst them being the following:—Chitoriáh, Máski, Rúchál, Húnchún, Thára, Láye, Tharáli, Súrjabansi or Súrajvansi, Hiski, and Masrángi.

The Thápá tribe is by far the greatest of all, and amongst them, yearly, hundreds of excellent recruits are obtained. Care should, however, be exercised in the selection of Thápás, as a very large number of men adopt the title of Thápá, although they have no right to the same.

The Sáru and Gáhá clans of the Thápá are each subdivided into five or more families, and in each case the Kálá family is the best.

The Púrána Gorakh Regiment in Nepál consists entirely of Magars, and is a splendid body of men. All the finest Magars of Nepál, excepting those in the Rifle regiments, are put into this regiment. They must be nearly if not quite as big as the Káli Bahádar.

MAGARS.

Allea Clans.

Arghúli or Arghounle.	Meng.
Biji.	Pacháin.
Cháng.	Palámi ⎫ probably the
Chármi.	Pulámi ⎭ same.
Dúkcháki.	Pangmi ⎫ probably the
	Púngmi ⎭ same.

Gar.
Gondá.
Gyangmi.
Húnchún.
Kalami.
Kháli.
Khaptari.
Kharri.
Khúlál.
Kilung.
Kúlángi.
Kiapcháki.
Lahakpá.
Lámchania.
Lamjál.
Limiál.
Lungchia.
Magiam.
Máski.

Panthi.
Pungi.
Phiwáli. { or Piwáli / or Phiúyáli.
Rakhál.
Ramial.
Ro.
Sarángi.
Serthúng.
Silthúng.
Sinjápati.
Sithúng { probably Silthúng.
Sripáli.
Súrajvansi or Súrjabansi.
Súyál.
Tarokche.
Thákcháki.
Yángmi.

Bárathoki Clans.

Balkoti.
Barkwánri.
Darlámi.
Deobal.
Gamál.
Karmani.
Lamichania.

Paháre or Pahária.
Ramjáli.
Ramkhani.
Ranjú.
Sinjápati.
Ulángia.

Chohán Clans. *

Gorá.
Kálá.

Thápá.

* As mentioned in my notes, I think the Choháns are not Magars at all, but Matwala Khas from the west of Nepál, although they will stoutly swear they are pure Magars. —E. V.

Gharti Clans.

Arghúli or Arghounle.
Baima.
Bainjáli.
Bhujiál.
Búlámi.
Chanchal } probably the
Chantial } same.
Dargánú.
Darlámi.
Galámi.
Gamál.
Giál.

Páre or Pária.
Púrja.
Ramjáli.
Rijál.
Rankami { (probably Rankhami).
Salámi.
Sámia.
Sáru.
Sawangi.
Senia.
Sinjáli.

Hunjáli.
Kahúcha.
Konsa.
Lámchania.
Masrángi.
Paháre or Pahária.

Sinjápati.
Sutpaháre.
Thein.
Tirgia.
Ulángia.
Wália.

*Jáli Clans.**

Atjáli.
Chárjáli.
Chejáli.
Dojáli.

Ekjáli.
Panchjali.
Sátjali.
Tinjáli.

* I came across three recruits belonging to the Jali Clans in 1889. But I have never heard of them before, nor can I find any mention of them in any book.—E. V.

Pún Clans.

Báijali.
Bapál.
Barángi.
Darlámi.
Dúd.
Húnjáli.
Tagonlia.
Kámi.
Paháre.
Pajánsi.
Phungáli.
Rákskoti.

Ramjáli.
Rángu.
Sáhi.
Samia.
Sarbúngá.
Sinjáli.
Sinjápati.
Sutpaháre.
Takália.
Támia.
Tirkhia.
Ulángia.

Rána Clans.

Archámi.
Arghúli or Arghounle.
Aslámi.
Bhúsál.
Byángnási.
Chármi.
Chitoriah.
Chúmi.
Darlámi.*
Dúd or Dút.
Durungcheng.
Gáchá.
Gandharmá.
Gyángmi.
Gyandris.
Hiski.
Húnchán.
Tiándi.
Kamcháki.
Kiapcháki.
Khiúyáli.

Bangling.
Barál or Balál.
Barkwánri.
Máski.
Masrángi.
Námjáli.
Panti.
Parta.
Phiwáli { or Piwáli / or Phiúyáli.
Pulámi.
Púsál (probably Bhúsál).
Rángú.
Reshmi.
Rúchál.
Sáru.
Sinjáli.
Sinjápati.
Súnári.
Súrajvansi or Súrjabansi.
Thárá or Thádá.

Lámchania.
Lungeli.
Láye.
Mákim.

Tháráli.
Uchai.
Yahayo.

* Perhaps this should be spelt Darra Lámi.—E. V.

Thápá Clans.

Allea.
Arghúli or Arghounle.
Aslámi.
Báchia or Bachio.
Bagália { Sátighari. Atghari.
Baigália.
Bailick.
Bákábal.
Balál or Barál.
Balámi.
Bankabarál.
Báola.
Báráhghari.
Bareya.
Barkwánri.
Bhomrel.

Biángmi.
Birkhatta.
Burathoki.
Chahári.
Charti.
Chídí.
Chitoriah.
Chúmi.
Dálá or Dáliá.
†Dárlámi { Bagália. Kálá.
Denga or Dhega.
Dengabúja.
Dengál.
Dishwa or Disuwá.
Durel.
Fál or Phál.

† Perhaps this should be spelt Darra Lámi. The Bagália Dárlámi is very good. E. V.

Gághá.
Gáhá { Kálá. Gorá. Barda. Badcha. Chidi.
Gáhab (probably Gáhá).
Gáncháki.
Garjá.
Garánjá.
Gelung.
Gidiel or Gindil.
Giángdi or Giámi.
Giánris.
Hiski.
Hithan.
Húnchún.
Ismálá.
Jargáh.
Jehári or Jhiádi.
Jhánkri or Jhangdi.
Jhenri.
Kaikalá.
Kámchá.

Mandir.
Masrángi.
Marúncha.
Máski.
Medun.
Mogmi.
Namjáli.
Pachbáyá.
Palli.
Pátá.
Pengmi.
Phál.
Phunjáli.
Phiwáli { or Piwali or Phiúyáli.
Powán.
Púánri.
Pulámi.
Rajvansi.
Rai.
Rájáli.
Rakál.
Rákskoti.
Ramjáli.

Kámú.
Kánhún (hard h).
Kánlú or Kánlúk.
Kanrdlu (same as Kánlú).
Kású.
Kejung.
Keli.
Khaptari.
Konwár.
Korál.
Kúlál.
Lámchania.
Lámtari.
Lánchiá.
Langakoti.
Langkang.
Láye.
Lungeli.
Mákim.
Mámring.
Súnári.
Súrajvansi or Súrjabansi.
Thagnámi.
Thámú.
Thárá or Thádá.

Ramkhani.
Rehári.
Reshmi.
Regámi.
Rijái.
Rúchál.
Sartúngi.
Sárú { Gorá. Jáparluk. Jhenri. Kálá. Malengia. Paneti. }
Sátighari.
Sinjáli.
Sinjápati.
Sirnia.
Sothi.
Súhnákhári.
Súmai or Some.
Thárún.
Thúrain.
Uchái.
Untaki or Wantaki.
Yángdi.

THÁKÚRS

Of all Goorkhás, excepting the Bráhman, the Thákúr has the highest social standing, and of all Thákúrs the Sáhi is the best. The Máhárája. Dhiráj (King of Nepál) is a Sáhi.

The Thákúr claims royal descent, and even to this day a really purebred Sáhi Thdku Thákúr is not charged rent for land in Nepál.

Thákúrs, on account of their high social standing, intelligence, cleanliness, and soldierly qualities, should invariably be taken if belonging to good clans. As soldiers they are excellent, and they can be obtained in small numbers, with quite as good physique and appearance as the best Magar or Gurung.

A Thákúr who has not adopted the thread, which until marriage is with him an entirely voluntary action, has no more prejudices than the ordinary Magar or Gurung, and even after adopting the thread his caste prejudices are not so very great, nor does he ever allow them to obtrude.

The Hamál Thákúr should not be enlisted by any regiment.

The best Thákúr clans are the following:—Sáhi, Malla, Sing, Sen, Khán, and Súmál.

The "Singála Uchái" is really a Sáhi by descent and is excellent, but all other Ucháis and the balance of Thákúr clans are not up to those above mentioned, although all Thákúr clans claim to be equal, with the exception of the Hamál. The Hamál is no Thákúr at all, but the progeny of an Opadia Bráhman with a Thákúr woman.

A Thákúr king, it is said, in the course of his conquests came to a very high hill called Singálá. This he captured from his enemies, and on the top of the same he established a garrison of Sáhi Thákúrs. These in time came to be spoken of as the "Uchái Thákúrs," from the fact of their living at a high elevation.

The clan Uchái will be found amongst many tribes, and is supposed to be derived from a similar reason.

With the exception of the Singálá. Uchái, all other Thákúr Ucháis are the progeny of a Thákúr with a Magar.

THÁKÚR CLANS.

Bam.	Mán.
Bansi.	Raika.
Chand.	Rakhsia.
Chohán (doubtful).	Rúchál.
Hamál.	Sáhi.
Jiú.	Sen.
Jiva.	Sing.
Khán.	Súmál.
Malla or Mal.	Uchái.

NEWÁRS.

The Newárs are not a warlike or military race, but there can be no doubt that they occasionally produce good soldiers.

The best Newár caste is the Sirisht, and one, Súbadár Kishnbir Nagarkoti, of the 5th Goorkhás, belonging to this caste, won the Order of Merit three times for gallantry displayed during the Kábul war, and was given a gold clasp when recommended a fourth time for conspicuous gallantry displayed at the time of Major Battye's death, in the Black Mountains, in 1888.

The Newárs also fought most bravely and in a most determined way against the Goorkhá conquerors—a fact proved by their twice defeating Prithvi Narain, as before mentioned.

They have letters and literature, and are well skilled in the useful and fine arts, having followed the Chinese and also Indian models; their agriculture is unrivalled in Népál, and their towns, temples, and images of the gods are beautiful, and unsurpassed in material and workmanship.

They are a steady, industrious people, and skilled in handicraft, commerce, and the culture of the earth.

The *Jaicis* are their priesthood and should never, on any account, be enlisted in our regiments.

Roughly speaking, the Limbús inhabit the eastern portion of Népál, and the Ráis the country between the Limbús and the valley of Népál. They are mostly cultivators or shepherds. Their physique is good, and in appearance they are much like an ordinary Magar or Gurung. They are very brave men, but of headstrong and quarrelsome natures, and, taken all round, are not considered as good soldiers as the Magar or Gurung.

There is one regiment of Limbús in the Népálese army, called the Bháiranáth, but on account of their quarrelsome natures they were always quartered apart. The Limbús are born *shikáris*, and most of the Máhárájáh's tiger-trackers are Limbús.

The writer knows very little about them so far, but hopes shortly to give a list of their clans. They are very desirable men, he hears.

RÁIS.

Kiránti Ráis.

Bantawár.	Khámbú.
Bútépá.	Kúlápáchá.
Debú.	Kulungia.
Dilipá.	Matwali.
Dobali.	Potrin.
Hatwáli.	Púwál.
Hondni.	Tánglúá.
Káling.	Thúlúng.
Kámtal.	Waling.

LINE-BOYS.

The progeny of Goorkhá soldiers, who are born an d brought up in the regiment, are called line-boys, and these might be divided into two distinct classes—

1. The progeny of purely Goorkhá parents.

2. The progeny of a Goorkhá soldier with a hill-woman. From the first class, if carefully selected, some excellent soldiers can be obtained.

The second class should be avoided. The pure-bred line-boy is just as intelligent as the half-bred, and if boys are required for the band, or men as clerks, &c., it would be better to select them from out of the first class.

Only a small percentage of line-boys, even of the first class, should be enlisted.

The claims of line-boys to be provided for in the service are undoubtedly very great, as Government has always, and very wisely too, encouraged Goorkhá colonies, and their fathers and grandfathers, having in many cases been all their lives in British employ, they have no other home than their regimental lines.

In their first generation their physique does not deteriorate much, and they almost invariably grow up to be extremely intelligent men and full of military ardour.

Their military education begins with their perceptive powers, as they commence playing at soldiers as soon as they can toddle about. The worst point against line-boys is that unfortunately they often prove to be men of very loose habits.

Sir Charles Reid, K.C.B., mentions that out of seven men who obtained the Order of Merit for the battles of Aliwal and Sobraon, five were line-boys; and out of twenty-five Order of Merit men for the siege of Delhi, twelve were line-boys.

The Kamárá is a slave. Most of the higher officials in Népál retain Kamárás as attendants.

The offspring of a Magar, Gurung, or Khas with a Kamárá would be a Kamárá.

Kwás is the offspring of a slave-mother with a Thákúr. The children of this union become Kwás, and their posterity retains the name. Kwás is also the name given to the illegitimate children of the King or Royal Family.

A Konwár who claims to be a Magar is the offspring of the connexion between a mendicant and any woman. He is generally an ill-bred-looking man, and should not be enlisted. The Khas Konwár is all right.

The Dhotias live in the extreme west of Népál, and south of Júmlá. They are not Goorkhás at all, and should never be enlisted.

Any man can become a *Bánda*, which practically means a bondsman. For instance, A will go to B and say, "Give me sixty *rupees* cash and I will be your *bánda* for two years."

On receipt of money he becomes a *bánda* and is bound to work for the two years for nothing beyond his food, but at the expiration of his two years, if he has contracted no fresh debt, he becomes free again.

MENIAL CLASSES.

The following is a list of some of the menial classes of Népál.

No man belonging to any of these should be enlisted as a soldier.

If it is found necessary to enlist any of them on account of their professional acquirements, they should be given separate quarters, and as far as possible be kept entirely away from all military duties.

Their being allowed to take their share as soldiers at guard-mounting, etc, etc., cannot raise, in the eyes of a real Goorkhá soldier, the glory of being a soldier.

Chamákhalá	Scavenger.
Damái	Tailor, Musician.
Drái	Seller of pottery.
Gáin	Bard.
Kamárá	Slave.
Kámi or Lohár	Ironsmith.
Kasái (Newár)	Butcher.
Kumhál	Potter.
Mánji	Boatman.
Pipa	Klasi.
Pore	Sweeper.
Sárkhi	Worker in leather.

SARKHI CLANS.

Workers in leather, a menial class.

Basiel.	Hitung.
Bhomrel.	Madkoti.
Bilekoti.	* Mangránti.
Chitoriah.	Ramtél.
Dankoti.	Rimál.
Gaire.	Sirketi.
Hamália.	Sirmal.

* This clan is derived from the fact of the ancestors of the same having resided within the Báráh Mangránth.—E. V.

PART 5

Recruiting

A brief description of how Goorkhá recruiting is carried out may perhaps not be out of place here.

A recruiting depot has been established in Gorakhpur.

Gorakhpur is on the River Rapti, and is the headquarters of the Bengal and North-Western Railway. It has an excellent central position with regard to Népál, as a line drawn at right angles, and dividing in half the length of Népál, would pass very close to Gorakhpur.

Gorakhpur is about 50 miles to the south of the nearest point of the Népál Terái.

The recruiting *depôt* consists of the following buildings:—Five regular double blocks (each double block consisting of two barracks), two irregular houses, four *baniahs'* shops, and one *chowkidar's* hut.

Government has this year (1889) sanctioned the building of two more barracks, and two sets of latrines. These will be erected during the coming cold weather.

One barrack is told off for the recruiting party of each Goorkha regiment, and in this are kept all the goods and chattels of the party, and all recruits enlisted are housed in the same until despatched to regimental headquarters.

Every year two British officers and one medical officer are told off for recruiting duty. They should be in Gorakhpur about the 1st October of every year.

Every regiment sends its own recruiting party, which generally consists of one Native officer, two or three non-commissioned officers, and a certain number of *sepoys*. The recruiting parties, if possible, should reach Gorakhpur before the end of October.

The Native officer of each party remains in Gorakhpur, keeping one non-commissioned officer or intelligent *sepoy* to assist.

One non-commissioned officer or steady soldier is sent to Tribeni Ghát, and one to Nautanwa.

Tribeni Ghát is on the east bank of the River Gandak, and is in British territory, although on the very edge of the Népál Terái. Tribeni is about 62 miles to the north-east of Gorakhpur, every foot of which has to be marched. Every year a fair (*mela*) is held here. Numbers of grass houses are erected, and crowds of villagers flock in to traffic. At this time a great many recruits are obtained.

Just opposite to Tribeni, and on the other side of the Gandak River, is the important village of Showpúr, which is in Népálese territory. Here a Népálese official always resides.

Nautanwa is a large village with a big *bazár*. It is in British territory, but within a mile or so of the Népá ese Terái, and only one long march from Botwál. Nautanwa is 54 miles to the north of Gorakhpur, but 20 miles of this journey can be done by rail, *viz.*, from Gorakhpur to Pharenda.

The non-commissioned officers at Tribeni and Nautanwa are given a certain amount of money, and are also provided with a measuring tape. The remainder of the party go off singly or otherwise into such portions of Népál as they think most likely to produce good recruits.

Any recruiter who has succeeded in getting a recruit, returns to the nearest *ghát*, *viz.*, to Tribeni or Nautanwa, as the case may be. The non-commissioned officer there examines the recruit as to tribe, clan, etc.: if this turns out satisfactory, he then measures him, and if up to the regimental standard, he sends him into Gorakhpur.

If any recruit brought up to the non-commissioned officer at either *ghát* turns out to be of an undesirable class, or to be under the regimental standard, he is turned back there and then, and the recruiter who brought him in loses all money expended in feeding the recruit. This serves the recruiter right, as he has no business to bring in an undesirable man.

The non-commissioned officers at the *ghát* should give advances of money where required. For instance, it often happens that a *sepoy* has gone perhaps ten days' journey or more to a distant village, in search of good material. He there perhaps finds, say, two recruits, whom he brings back all the way to the nearest *ghát*. He has to feed himself and the two lads all the journey, and very probably arrives at the *ghát* stone broke. The non-commissioned officer thereupon should give the man sufficient money to ensure his being able to feed himself and his recruits as far as Gorakhpur.

Any recruit brought in to Gorakhpur is made over to the Native officer commanding the party to which the recruiter belongs. The Native officer enquires about the lad's tribe, clan, village, etc.; then measures him, and if all proves satisfactory, he then causes the recruit's hair to be cut, makes him bathe from head to foot, and the next morning brings him up to the British officer on recruiting duty.

The British officer enquires about his tribe, clan, etc., and then measures him. If all proves satisfactory, he then enters his name in the nominal roll, and sends the lad on to the medical officer, who, having ascertained his fitness for the service, enters all remarks opposite the recruit's name.

When ten to twelve recruits have been medically passed for any regiment, they are despatched to headquarters in charge of a *sepoy*.

In 1888 Government sanctioned the giving of rewards to *sepoys* for every really fine recruit brought in.

The recruiting officer was allowed to fix his own standard of rewards. As the object of giving rewards was to get the best possible recruits, he determined that no reward should be paid to any soldier for any recruit who was under 5' 2" in height or whose chest was less than 32" in girth.

The bigger the recruit, the greater the reward given, as long as his tribe, clan, etc., proved thoroughly satisfactory.

The importance of sending good recruiting agents to Gorakhpur cannot be overestimated. If they are good men and hard workers, the results will be good recruits, and plenty of them.

Recruiting agents should be men either picked out on account of former success on recruiting duty or because they appear suited by nature for this work.

Young soldiers, as a rule, are not so successful as those over five or six years' service.

Any senior non-commissioned officer or soldier who is likely to receive his promotion shortly, and who at the same time seems suited for recruiting duty, might with advantage be sent on the same, being promised his promotion if he does well.

When selecting a recruiting party, the greatest care should be taken in ascertaining that the men composing the same belong to different districts or *tehsils*.

A man from each of the following *tehsils* might with advantage be selected:—Baglúng, Garhúng, Lámjúng, Káski, Galkot Gúlmi, Pokra, Bhirkot, Goorkhá, Pálpa, Kánchi, and Argha.

A recruiter will generally go straight to his own village- By picking out men belonging to different *tehsils*, we get our agents over most of the good recruiting grounds, and not limited to a few districts only. Every recruiter should be provided with a measuring tape or string long enough to show the minimum height and chest measurement required for his regiment.

By giving these tapes, the recruiters are saved coming in long distances, only to find their recruits rejected as being under the standard required.

The Native officer commanding the recruiting party should be given ample funds. The want of cash often loses recruits. To explain the reason of this would take too much space, but it nevertheless remains a fact, and any party that has insufficient funds, or is kept waiting for money, will suffer thereby.

Every Native officer should be provided with a sufficient number of blankets, to enable him to give one to each recruit prior to despatch to headquarters. Gorakhpur is very much hotter than any of our Goorkhá stations, and if a recruit is sent to join his regiment, say in December, he will most undoubtedly suffer from the cold if unprovided with a blanket.

Each Native officer should be given a bottle or two filled with quinine pills. By sending some of these pills to the *gháts*, and dosing recruits and soldiers with them, before and after going through the Terái, a deal of fever is saved.

The Native officer should in every way encourage his party to work, and should keep himself as far as possible informed as to what each recruiter is doing. Recruiters are much too fond of lounging about big *bazárs*, such as Botwál and Showpúr, on the chance of picking up recruits there. They should be directed not to do this, but to go right away to distant villages.

The best recruits are generally those who have been brought in direct from their villages.

It often happens, too, that some of the recruiters, being of amorous dispositions, will devote their time to the fascinations of some fair being, instead of climbing up and down hills, looking for recruits. It is the business of the Native officer to find this out, and to put a stop to their blandishments.

An impression seemed at one time to exist that the yearly demand for Goorkhá recruits was greater than the supply.

The writer of this, having had much experience in recruiting duty at Gorakhpur, ventures to give his opinion upon the same. He thinks that, if Goorkhás were kept solely and entirely for enlistment into the regular army, there would be no difficulty whatsoever in every year getting the full requirements.

Now that all the second battalions are quite complete, the requirements of Goorkhi regiments serving in India will be on an average about fifty recruits per regiment *per annum*.

The three regiments serving in Assam during the past three years enlisted 1,034 recruits, or, roughly speaking, 120 per regiment *per annum*.

The annual requirements would therefore be, say, as follows:—

	Recruits.
9 Regiments in India, at 50 per regiment	450
3 Do. in Assam at 120 ,,	360
Total annual requirements	810

Make a liberal allowance and say the annual requirement is 900 recruits.

This number, the writer feels convinced, could easily be obtained every year, *as long as no obstructions are thrown in our way by the Népálese officials*. This is a *sine quâ non*.

During the 1888-89 season the following results were obtained:—

By Goorkhá Regiments serving in India,

Number of Recruits enlisted.	Age in years.	Average Height	Chest
509	18.59	5' 3.75"	33.88"

By Goorkhá Regiments serving in Assam,

Number of Recruits enlisted.	Age in years.	Average Height	Chest
363	18.05	5' 2.50"	33.10"

For the whole Army,

Number of Recruits enlisted.	Age in years.	Average Height	Chest
872	18.37	5' 3.21"	33.56"

This will give a very fair idea of what the average ought to be of any squad of recruits. If course some men will be a good deal above and some a good deal below these measurements, but the average of most squads should be up to the same.

It will be noticed that the average of the physique of recruits for the Assam regiments is a good deal smaller than for the rest of the Goorkhá regiments, but this is due to their requirements every year being so very much greater. During the 1888-89 season all regiments got their full complement, and all got one hundred *per cent*, of Magars and Gurungs, excepting such regiments as gave special orders for a limited number of lads of other castes.

FURLOUGH MEN.

When granting warrants to furlough men, it should be remembered that all Goorkhás serving in India will require double warrants,—*viz.*, one from headquarters to Ajúdhiá Ghát, and one from Lakarmandi to destination,—*viz.*, to Népálganj or Báláganj, to Gorakhpur or Pharenda, as the case may be.

The Oudh and Rohilkhand Railway is a broad-gauge line and runs as far as Ajúdhiá Ghát, on the banks of the Gogra River.

This river is crossed either by means of a steam-ferry or by a bridge of boats, and on the other bank is the Bengal and North-Western Railway Station called Lakarmandi. This is a narrow-gauge line.

From Lakarmandi the line runs to a junction called Mankapur, where one branch line goes off west by north-west to Népálganj, and the other branch goes off east to Gorakhpur, and through Gorakhpur due north on to Pharenda and Uska Bazár.

Pharenda is the nearest railway station to Nautanwa, and consequently to Botwál.

For the three Assam regiments, in addition to the warrants by steamer, only one railway warrant is required,—*viz.*, from Dhubri *viâ* Naihatti to destination,—*viz.*, to Gorakhpur, or Pharenda, or Népálganj, as the case may be.

Furlough men can immensely assist recruiting operations by bringing in a recruit or two with them on their return from furlough. They should be urged to do so prior to their starting for their homes.

Most furlough men return from their homes very hard up. Numbers of them, on their arrival at Gorakhpur on their return journey, apply to the recruiting officer for an advance. The recruiting officer has no funds available for this purpose. Commanding officers who desire that their men should be given small advances, when absolutely necessary, might with great advantage send a certain amount of money to the recruiting officer for this purpose.

At present men are kept waiting for a long while until the money has been applied for, and received from headquarters. This leads to a great deal of extra correspondence, and to considerable delay.

This applies especially to regiments serving in Assam, as it takes a long while getting money from thence.

If money were sent to the recruiting officer for the purpose of giving advances, he should only give the same where absolutely necessary, and would submit an account of how the money was expended, after all furlough men had returned.

ALSO FROM LEONAUR
AVAILABLE IN SOFTCOVER OR HARDCOVER WITH DUST JACKET

FARAWAY CAMPAIGN *by F. James*—Experiences of an Indian Army Cavalry Officer in Persia & Russia During the Great War.

REVOLT IN THE DESERT *by T. E. Lawrence*—An account of the experiences of one remarkable British officer's war from his own perspective.

MACHINE-GUN SQUADRON *by A. M. G.*—The 20th Machine Gunners from British Yeomanry Regiments in the Middle East Campaign of the First World War.

A GUNNER'S CRUSADE *by Antony Bluett*—The Campaign in the Desert, Palestine & Syria as Experienced by the Honourable Artillery Company During the Great War.

DESPATCH RIDER *by W. H. L. Watson*—The Experiences of a British Army Motorcycle Despatch Rider During the Opening Battles of the Great War in Europe.

TIGERS ALONG THE TIGRIS *by E. J. Thompson*—The Leicestershire Regiment in Mesopotamia During the First World War.

HEARTS & DRAGONS *by Charles R. M. F. Crutwell*—The 4th Royal Berkshire Regiment in France and Italy During the Great War, 1914-1918.

INFANTRY BRIGADE: 1914 *by John Ward*—The Diary of a Commander of the 15th Infantry Brigade, 5th Division, British Army, During the Retreat from Mons.

DOING OUR 'BIT' *by Ian Hay*—Two Classic Accounts of the Men of Kitchener's 'New Army' During the Great War including *The First 100,000 & All In It*.

AN EYE IN THE STORM *by Arthur Ruhl*—An American War Correspondent's Experiences of the First World War from the Western Front to Gallipoli-and Beyond.

STAND & FALL *by Joe Cassells*—With the Middlesex Regiment Against the Bolsheviks 1918-19.

RIFLEMAN MACGILL'S WAR *by Patrick MacGill*—A Soldier of the London Irish During the Great War in Europe including *The Amateur Army, The Red Horizon & The Great Push*.

WITH THE GUNS *by C. A. Rose & Hugh Dalton*—Two First Hand Accounts of British Gunners at War in Europe During World War 1- Three Years in France with the Guns and With the British Guns in Italy.

THE BUSH WAR DOCTOR *by Robert V. Dolbey*—The Experiences of a British Army Doctor During the East African Campaign of the First World War.

AVAILABLE ONLINE AT **www.leonaur.com**
AND FROM ALL GOOD BOOK STORES

ALSO FROM LEONAUR
AVAILABLE IN SOFTCOVER OR HARDCOVER WITH DUST JACKET

THE 9TH—THE KING'S (LIVERPOOL REGIMENT) IN THE GREAT WAR 1914 - 1918 by Enos H. G. Roberts—Mersey to mud—war and Liverpool men.

THE GAMBARDIER by Mark Severn—The experiences of a battery of Heavy artillery on the Western Front during the First World War.

FROM MESSINES TO THIRD YPRES by Thomas Floyd—A personal account of the First World War on the Western front by a 2/5th Lancashire Fusilier.

THE IRISH GUARDS IN THE GREAT WAR - VOLUME 1 by Rudyard Kipling—Edited and Compiled from Their Diaries and Papers—The First Battalion.

THE IRISH GUARDS IN THE GREAT WAR - VOLUME 1 by Rudyard Kipling—Edited and Compiled from Their Diaries and Papers—The Second Battalion.

ARMOURED CARS IN EDEN by K. Roosevelt—An American President's son serving in Rolls Royce armoured cars with the British in Mesopatamia & with the American Artillery in France during the First World War.

CHASSEUR OF 1914 by Marcel Dupont—Experiences of the twilight of the French Light Cavalry by a young officer during the early battles of the great war in Europe.

TROOP HORSE & TRENCH by R.A. Lloyd—The experiences of a British Lifeguardsman of the household cavalry fighting on the western front during the First World War 1914-18.

THE EAST AFRICAN MOUNTED RIFLES by C.J. Wilson—Experiences of the campaign in the East African bush during the First World War.

THE LONG PATROL by George Berrie—A Novel of Light Horsemen from Gallipoli to the Palestine campaign of the First World War.

THE FIGHTING CAMELIERS by Frank Reid—The exploits of the Imperial Camel Corps in the desert and Palestine campaigns of the First World War.

STEEL CHARIOTS IN THE DESERT by S. C. Rolls—The first world war experiences of a Rolls Royce armoured car driver with the Duke of Westminster in Libya and in Arabia with T.E. Lawrence.

WITH THE IMPERIAL CAMEL CORPS IN THE GREAT WAR by Geoffrey Inchbald—The story of a serving officer with the British 2nd battalion against the Senussi and during the Palestine campaign.

AVAILABLE ONLINE AT **www.leonaur.com**
AND FROM ALL GOOD BOOK STORES

www.ingramcontent.com/pod-product-compliance
Lightning Source LLC
Chambersburg PA
CBHW021003090426
42738CB00007B/637